I dedicate this book to my late father, Clevelon Marshall, and to my offspring, Jasmine, Orlando, Dazarae, and Richard III. I also want to thank my mother, Alleta Bronaugh, Chief Allen Banks and the Round Rock Police Department, and all of my students over the years at Funny Bone Defensive Driving Class.

I have only just a minute,
Only sixty seconds in it.
Forced upon me, can't refuse it.
Didn't seek it, didn't choose it.
But it's up to me
to use it.
I must suffer if I lose it.
Give account if I abuse it.
Just a tiny little minute,
but eternity is in it.
—Dr. Benjamin Mays

Isabella

Be blessed, thank you for your support. I wish you great things in life.

CONSEQUENCES AND COMPASSION

LESSONS FROM THE FRONTLINES OF DRUNK, DRUGGED, AND DISTRACTED DRIVING

LaDONNA CLAUDE

HOUNDSTOOTH
PRESS

CONSEQUENCES AND COMPASSION
Lessons from the Frontlines of Drunk, Drugged, and Distracted Driving

ISBN   HARDCOVER: 978-1-5445-3767-2
       PAPERBACK: 978-1-5445-3676-7
       EBOOK: 978-1-5445-3677-4

CONTENTS

PREFACE

I have worked as an instructor at Texas's Funny Bone Defensive Driving for more than seven years, and I am always thinking about driving. Specifically, I am always thinking about DWI—*driving while impaired*. During my classes, I can tell that my students are connecting with what I say. After all, many of them are there hoping to have their tickets dismissed. The information I share makes sense to them, and even if they don't leave my class perfect (because *no one* is perfect), every student has learned something by the time they return to their day-to-day lives.

Over time, I've started to describe the destruction we cause when we receive a DWI as *setting a fire*. These flames can grow to engulf not only you but everyone and everything around you. This destruction is prohibitively expensive. If I can help just one person decide not to strike that match, then I have done something worthwhile.

This means so much to me because I have seen flames that have burned lives to the ground. I am personally familiar with the gut-wrenching feeling of looking all around and seeing only fire, choking on the smoke. I know what can happen in these situations and how quickly they can spiral out of control.

Still, I want to make it clear that my intention is *never* to judge anyone. To me, love and forgiveness are the only ways of life. I believe that God is love, which is why *I love you too*. It is not my role to stand in judgment of you. That is not what this book is about.

This book is about consequences. It is a careful examination of a hundred different reasons not to light a DWI match and set the life you know on fire. My intention is to carry over the valuable information I uncovered and discussed in the classes that I've taught. Every class I have taught has motivated me to share my thoughts in this format. I am eager to share what I know but first, I want to warn you that as you read, it may get intense. This book may open your eyes to things that you haven't considered or acknowledged before. For me, learning this information was a revelation; one that helped me see that we are *all* a part of this.

It is important to mention that this book is *not* going to try to convince you to stop drinking or abusing drugs. While I don't drink or use drugs, I believe you have a right to choose whether or not to do so. It is up to you. This is your life to plan and your life to live. My goal is to provide you with information and a second perspective, so you understand the consequences of your choices and your actions.

As you read this book, you may develop some questions. Do I think this person or that one *deserves* a DWI? Do I have compassion for everyone who gets a DWI? Yes, I do! As you read, I hope you realize where I stand. Whatever the case, know that these are simply my thoughts based on years of study and reflection. Facts are always key in any case, and the details of DWI laws can update or change. Revisions happen *often*, and to stay up to date, you need to keep learning too.

EVERYBODY IS SOMEBODY

In an instant, your life can change. As it so happens, an instant is exactly how long it takes for a lot of people in our society to decide your life doesn't hold value any longer. One and done: that is what they think about mistakes, especially mistakes like a DWI that can cause harm.

Before I go any further, I want to clear up a point that commonly confuses people: the difference between a DUI and a DWI. The reason this point is so confusing is that the terms are used differently from one jurisdiction to the next. Some states use the term "DUI" across the board, while others use the term "DWI." In Texas, we say that a DUI is for someone under the age of twenty-one. A DWI is, on the other hand, for someone over the age of twenty-one. DWI stands for "Driving While Impaired," and DUI stands for "Driving Under the Influence." Other people refer to a DUI *only* when there is alcohol involved.

For the sake of simplicity, I am going to use the term "DWI" throughout this book. I will frequently talk about the "three Ds" of DWI, which are *driving*, *drugs*, and *distraction*. Any of these things can lead to a car accident, and any of these things can lead to a criminal charge.

As an aside, if you are under the age of twenty-one in Texas, then the local "minor consumption" laws apply to you. These are *not* free passes. If you plead guilty to a DUI, you are subject to almost all the same penalties that would fall upon someone who got a DWI. The only difference is that the judge is more likely to consider your eligibility for pre-trial programs to avoid jail time and a criminal record.

If you or someone you care about has been injured due to someone else's DWI, I feel for you. I have read about and heard about so many of these cases. I am all too familiar with the pain and strife they can cause. It sometimes seems that hurt sticks with you for the rest of your life. No matter what you do, you can't seem to shake off the weight of what has happened to you. As a result, you look for someone to blame. You lash out, understandably, at the person who was driving when they should not have been.

However, know that in this book, I am going to show some of the Christian compassion I believe everyone deserves. As difficult as it is to see the world from that perspective; as challenging as it may be to understand that mistakes happen and all we can do is pick up the pieces and move on; I am going to ask you to try to do that. Try to think about what life is like for *the other person*, for the one who was driving that day, for the one who caused you harm when you were only minding your own business.

Time and again, I have seen evidence of this truth: everybody is somebody. Each of us has something to offer in this world—even if that is only the beauty of our spirit that our Creator has endowed us.

Compassion comes naturally to us all. It is our birthright. All of our lives have meaning. We can all step up, when necessary, to do more than we ever thought possible in the past.

There will be times when you are reading this book, especially if you are navigating the post-DWI process, where you may feel down or self-critical—when you may struggle to show *yourself* compassion. I am not going to hold anything back, because I believe it is important for you to receive all of this information. Still, I am not going to wear you down and give you nothing to build yourself back up. I am going to list the consequences and the realities inherent to the post-DWI process, as well as actions that you can take to change your life for the better. You can pick up the pieces and do something different from now on.

As a defensive driving instructor, I frequently meet people when they are at their low points. My number-one duty is to impart my knowledge to my students and to clear up any misconceptions they may hold about driving, drinking, drugs, and distraction. I also take on the role of motivational speaker, counselor, and evangelist. When one of my students needs to unload their burden and talk about what is going on for them, I feel a responsibility to listen to them. I make an effort to hear all they are trying to say, and I respond to them as kindly and helpfully as I can.

When I started working as a defensive driving instructor, I was not teaching any classes about DWI. However, DWI topics were always part of the curriculum. I spoke about those topics as a matter of overall safety. I took on the role and responsibility of teaching the DWI class itself when I realized I could provide real insight to people who were going through a tough time in their lives.

A year or two into my first DWI class, I started to write down the lessons I wanted to repeat for the class that came next. At first, there were only five or six items on this list of topics. Whenever my students and I talked about something new, I added to it, paying the most attention to topics that were causing my students the most problems.

In every one of these formative classes, the students would blurt things out, asking me to talk about various DWI subjects. Sometimes, the students guided the conversation themselves, telling me how they felt about one thing or another or explaining why something about the post-DWI process was perplexing for them. The list grew, little by little, and after seven or so years in front of my DWI classes, the list had reached *one hundred* items.

It was then that I thought I might be able to turn the list into something more, and my students encouraged me to do just that. Their reviews were always so positive and uplifting. In a system that seemed designed to push them back and hold them down, my classes were doing the opposite. I was able to point my students toward brighter days. When they sounded discouraged, I would tell them success stories. I would highlight a student whose situation had been *even worse* and who had nonetheless beaten the odds.

One of the first and most important things I want people to know is this: most wildfires aren't started on purpose. Still, the responsibility rests with the person who struck the match, no matter their reason for doing it. Some fires, while alarming, might be manageable and stopped, but others are uncontrollable. Sometimes they rage on and on, try as you might to smother the flames. Soon, the fire leaps from your immediate area to everything around it, multiplying like a virus and engulfing everything around you.

It is at this point that people realize the wildfire presents a danger not only to them personally, but to everyone and everything around them too. The personal reason you chose to drive while impaired is suddenly and easily dwarfed by the destructive flames that now threaten your security and relationships with loved ones, your home, your career, your community, and more.

As a reminder, the information in this book primarily applies to people in Texas. That is where I live and where I have done my research. State to state, the costs and the associated details will vary somewhat. However, these issues are relevant in all fifty states. Drinking, drugs, and distractions (the three types of "D" in "DWI") are an issue. There are laws that apply to people in every state, and in a real way, we are in the middle of an epidemic, costing lives, money, and order.

We all know, on some level, what happens when people fail to acknowledge the consequences of their actions. I have heard it all many times before. The regret sinks in until it pours out: "I'm sorry," and "I didn't mean to," or "How is this happening?" "Why me?" None of that anguish means anything to the police officer who pulled you over, though. At that moment, there is a fire blazing around you already. It can feel surreal, like a scene from a movie. It's lights, camera, action, and your only lines are the answers you manage to give when the officer asks how much you have had to drink and if you know how fast you were going.

When you walk the asphalt catwalk, there's an invisible fire following your footsteps. Everything you say and do is recorded on paper and on film. It'll be there for your big break when they add it all to the evidence pile at the local precinct. Were you high from prescription or nonprescription drugs? Did you have one drink or four? Were you answering your phone or gazing off at the sunset?

Think about that last question. As mentioned earlier, *yes*, the

"D" in "DWI" can stand for *distraction*. If your distraction is severe enough, it can land you in trouble similar to what you would be facing for drinking or drugs. Billboards and advertisements are *everywhere*. Our phones are never too far from our hands, either. We know that we need to keep our eyes on the road, yet too often, we simply don't.

As an experienced instructor and advocate for making informed, safe choices, I know it is my duty to talk to you about all of this. I have to start uncomfortable conversations like this one for the greater good. It isn't because I don't get it; I *do* get it. The sweet taste of wine, the temptation of an incoming text, and the relaxation of a springtime sunset. It is enough to overwhelm anyone, but each of those things are more similar to a lit match than most people realize. Fire can be hypnotic, and what happens next, as a consequence of creating those flames, is probably not worth the resulting inferno.

As you read this book, remember that no one is invincible. If you think this couldn't happen to you, you are wrong, and if you are beating yourself up because it already has happened to you, remind yourself that you are not alone. There is no culture, no social status, no age, no height, no race, and no size that escapes the impact of DWIs. We are *all* in this together.

Sadly, many people refuse to consider the consequences until they are right in the middle of them. We have all done that at one time or another, ignoring our situation until it becomes unbearable and unavoidable. What you need to do, though, is refuse to carry on in that way. You need to tell yourself that you are going to be different.

That may seem tough, but I know you're up to it. I have seen many others face themselves. No, we are not going to change the world, at least not overnight. We can change each of ourselves, however. *You* can decide that you are going to be different. If you recognize how important change is, then you can make it happen no matter how uncomfortable it is.

I want to open your eyes to your own life, to what makes it up, and what doesn't. Self-pity and denial? No, those are not your life. Your life is a matter of what you choose and decide, how you walk from one day to the next, the situations that you embrace, and the ones that you avoid.

By the time an officer or a court gets involved, you have already set some part of your life on fire. You may be able to withstand the heat, even for a very long time, but there is an easier way to go about things. Strengthening your awareness *right now*, cutting down on the liquor, or coming up with a responsible consumption plan are all valid ways you can start stomping out the flames.

The truth is this: you cannot afford a DWI because *no one* can. Without ever meeting you, without ever learning a single thing about your finances, your background, your goals, or your aspirations, I can tell you that a DWI would change your life for the worse. Think about what you owe to *yourself*. You need to take charge in your life and make the right decisions, especially in risky situations, such as any situation where alcohol is involved.

Remember that on every container of alcohol, it says, "Consumption of alcoholic beverages impairs your ability to drive a car or operate machinery." The bottlers put that warning there for a reason: they are protecting themselves. These companies understand the risks and dangers associated with consuming their product, and by warning you, the responsibility shifts from them to you. You need to be wise about all of this, and I can help you figure out how to do that.

CHAPTER I

The officer pulls you over. After you roll down the window, she explains to you that she suspects you of drinking or drug use. That is her probable cause to arrest you. Next, pending a field sobriety test, you are facing a night or more in jail. This is where your life changes. At this point, the wildfire becomes more than just a concept for you. The temperature starts rising immediately, and the fire becomes *very* real.

Let's go through the first ten possible consequences of receiving a DWI. This should help you develop an idea of how much fun you are (not) going to have. As you can see, things can heat up quickly.

1. JAIL

You drink; you drive; you go to jail. It has been that way for years. If you have never been behind bars before, ask anyone who has. They will tell you that it does *not* feel good. No one wants to spend a night in a closed, confined area. You wake up when the sheriff's deputies tell you to wake up. They also tell you when and what you eat, and then at the end of the day, they tell you when to sleep. You start to realize that freedom, just like fresh air, is a necessity in life. Living behind a locked door, you learn a lot about yourself. All the while, you are missing out on wages and perhaps even losing your job.

Waking up in jail and sleeping off a headache on a slab of concrete will help you realize beyond a doubt that you have made the wrong decision. Cultivate responsible habits around driving *before* that happens.

2. TOW TRUCK

Because you are unable to drive your car away from the scene of your DWI arrest, you have to pay for a tow-truck driver to come and pick it up. That will entail another charge, amounting to anywhere from $75 to $200. That bill follows you too. If you drive a truck or an SUV, it will cost even more because tow-truck drivers charge according to the size of your vehicle.

What is my advice here? The solution to a high tow-truck bill isn't to drive a smaller car, nor is it to give up driving altogether and stick with your bicycle. Instead, every time you pass a tow truck on the road, associate it in your mind with all the costs of a DWI. This mental exercise is going to reinforce proper, healthy thought patterns regarding driving.

No tow truck is merely a tow truck after reframing its significance in this way. You see someone towing a car, and you can recall what you are reading in these pages. Think about the damage that a DWI can cause. Simultaneously, think about all the wonderful things you can do with your life by staying out of trouble and keeping your driving record squeaky clean.

3. IMPOUND

Once your car is impounded, you must then pay another $300, plus $100 every day until you pick it up. You can't argue with any of that; this is a business, and your feelings do not count for anything. Think of the impound as a jail for your car, except instead of sentencing your car to a certain number of days or weeks, the impound refuses any release until you have paid your entire debt. There is never any guarantee that your car will be in a nearby impound, either. Impounds are frequently in more remote areas.

I will impart two pieces of advice to you here. First, in the event that your car does get impounded, don't waste any time picking it up. Get your car off the lot as soon as possible so you can minimize the costs you incur. Do the math: after a month in impound, many older, more modest vehicles would be "totaled," costing more to retrieve than their fair-market value.

Second, treat your car as if it is *sacred*. Frequently, people who get a DWI will face other charges for things like open-container violations and drug possession. Instead of putting yourself in that position, never do or carry anything in your car that can land you in trouble with the law.

4. COURT COSTS

In Texas, you will pay a minimum of $100 anytime you need to show up for a court date. More often than not, that cost is going to be higher. Civil and criminal courts will each tack on their own fees and charges so that, by the end of your case, you may have to agree to some sort of a payment plan with them. The point is that going to court is not going to be free. As much as you don't want to be there, you have to show up, and you have to cover the costs.

Lawyers attend law school for a reason: this stuff is *complicated*. A century or two ago, many jurisdictions would permit lawyers to teach themselves. These so-called "country lawyers"—President Lincoln was one—are no more. Again, there is a reason state bars want their lawyers to go to school, and that is because laws are too convoluted, and the stakes are too high, to leave people to their own devices.

Still, it does not hurt to *try* to learn a thing or two. I recommend studying up on the law as much as you can. Hopefully, you will never have to use this knowledge. When you are in a difficult situation, though, you will be grateful that you have studied up.

5. BAIL

Are there "Get Out of Jail Free" cards in life, like the ones in Monopoly? Technically, no. There is bail though. Bail, unlike those cards, does not come from a lucky roll of the dice, and it *certainly* isn't free. Instead, a family member or friend has to pay for it. They must post a certain amount of money as insurance, and if you fail to show up to your court date, they lose that insurance in its entirety. In most cases, a judge will set your bail somewhere from $1,000 to $10,000 and up, depending on the severity of the DWI and your perceived flight risk.

The best plan with regards to DWI is not to get one in the first place. However, the second-best plan is to *know* what you are going to do if the first plan breaks down. In this case, know whom you can call in an emergency. Paying bail is a hassle, but it is better than staying in jail.

Who in your life would respond to that three-in-the-morning phone call? If you are unsure, ask a few people who matter the most to you, just in case.

6. BONDSMAN

This is the gentleman or lady who is "selling" you that "Get Out of Jail" card. The keyword here is "selling" because *nothing* is free. When your bondsman posts your bail in exchange for the 10 percent or 20 percent deposit your loved one is paying, he or she expects that you are going to show up for court. He or she will also require you to sign a contract and put collateral in place. This will be something valuable, like a car or a house. Otherwise, the bondsman is on the hook for the whole bond. You can bet when that happens, your interaction with the bondsman is not going to come to a simple or friendly conclusion. You will find yourself in a situation where the bondsman is seeking you out. On top of that, you will be violating the trust that your bondsman has placed in you.

There is a Bible verse relevant to this, Proverbs 22:1: "A good name is to be chosen rather than great riches, loving favor rather than silver and gold."

I always feel frustrated when I hear about someone skipping out on bail. While bondsmen may not be the most popular people in their towns, they serve a real purpose and perform a meaningful service. Respect that! As a rule, you should live your life this way. That is what it means to choose a good name, as it is written in the book of Proverbs. Choose your good name again and again, abiding by the rules of decency that you would hope other people abide by.

7. ATTORNEY

Attorneys may be some of the best friends you will ever make. That has been the case for me, anyway. Several of my friends are attorneys, and seeing them work, I would say the ones who are most effective are the ones who are most passionate. The thing is, the passionate attorneys usually *know* how effective they are. In turn, they command hefty fees for their services. They know they are able to speak for the voiceless and defend the defenseless, navigating court cases much more smoothly than the majority of their peers. Your budget will decide if you can afford that type of lawyer or not. There is no quick menu for attorney fees, which means—you can assume—they are *expensive*. Run out of money and their representation comes to a screeching halt. It's nothing personal. Like the tow-truck driver and the bondsman, attorneys are in a business. They're trying to earn a living, and if they can do so while helping you, they will. Otherwise, they won't.

When it comes to attorneys, you *have* to do your research. In every major city across the country, there are attorneys who have barely held on to their credentials. They run flashy advertisements—or *less* flashy advertisements, played ad nauseam—to attract their clients. Many of them specialize in DWIs, and while it is best to hire some lawyer rather than no lawyer, this is not something to leave up to chance.

As always, you are better off doing your research *beforehand*. Decide whom you would call in an emergency. That is always a good idea anyway!

8. PUBLIC DEFENDER

What if you *can't* afford an attorney? Not the ones that say "$" for the price and certainly not the ones that say "$$$$" for the price. The court, because of the Sixth Amendment in the US Constitution's Bill of Rights, will then appoint an attorney to represent you free of charge. As the saying goes, of course, *you get what you pay for*. A free attorney knows the law, sure. They may offer you *some* assistance. By and large, though, their representation will fall far short of what you could have expected from an attorney in private practice. Plus, you are paying their salary through your taxes.

There is *no shame* in working with a public defender. Remember that when you are at your lowest point.

9. PROBATION OFFICER

After your case, once you have struck a plea bargain with the district attorney or once the court has found you guilty, the court will assign you a probation officer. Every month, like clockwork, you have to visit with your probation officer. They will show up when you least expect them to, even when it is least convenient, and they may request a urine sample analysis. This can happen while you are at your job or at your home. If there are drug tests, you may have guessed the following already: they will not be free. You have to pay for any tests and any probation visits. Violate the terms of your probation and you are even worse off, starting the process over again or even spending more time in jail.

I have known probation officers. Some of them are the kindest, best professionals I have met in my life. If you ask the people in their charge, however, you may not get the most glowing reviews. Remember that when you are working within the system. As stressful as it may be for you, probation officers and every other government official is *also* a human being. Show them respect and compassion, and you should be able to expect the same in return.

10. PROBATION ITSELF

When a judge orders you to go on probation for a period lasting from three to twenty-four months and beyond, you will be paying for all of that as well. Even if you never violate the terms of your probation, you are responsible for paying for it.

My suggestion here is only for those who are navigating post-DWI procedures. From the beginning, write everything down. Open up Excel or Numbers, create a fresh spreadsheet, and record what you spend and what you need to save. This way, something like probation—the costs of which will mount rapidly—will not send you into even more catastrophic circumstances.

A close friend of mine, James Gamble, who works as a probation officer said the following, "When one is on probation, from their lawyer's conversations, they are under the impression that they can serve half the probation period as long as they do their community service and pay fees and fines. That is an incorrect statement from the lawyer. For a DWI, your sentence will be twelve months to ten years. 'Adjudicated' means that it won't go away. It is always on your record, and you have to complete the whole term."

My friend went on to say, "Any defendant that comes to me that starts probation and is serving probation due to alcohol or drugs, I advise them not to drink or do drugs while on probation. From this point on and at each visit, there will be a urinalysis test. If you can't pay fees, pay something. That shows you care."

Of course, you may not be able to access a probation officer *before* you meet the probation officer who handles your case. That means you won't be able to get helpful advice like this. To prepare for your first meeting with your probation officer, talk with someone else who has worked with a probation officer and get a feel for the dos and don'ts.

CHAPTER II

To understand why I feel so passionately about this topic, you need to understand my father. He was a social drinker, which affected him in a number of ways for many years. In 2011, when my family was putting on a family reunion, I reached out to him but didn't get an answer. That was Sunday. The next day, I called again, and it was the same thing: no answer. Later that day, my half-sister called me to tell me the news.

He had passed away.

My father was gone, just like that. Unspeakably vulnerable as he wasted away, he was alone too, which is something that no one wants.

The reason I tell this story is to highlight that you don't know everyone's story. If you had met my father while he was alive and seen how much he struggled with his alcoholism, you might have drawn some conclusions about his death. It was much more than that, though. I don't think it would be fair to summarize him into a single event, just as I don't think it would be fair to summarize anyone else into a single DWI.

To anyone who didn't know him, my father may have seemed like a nobody. But as I've said before, *nobodies* don't exist. He was somebody. He was my father.

It's important to remember you don't know everyone's story. This is one of the reasons why maintaining compassion is so important to me.

Take the story of a twenty-year-old woman who walked into my class. When she got her DWI, it was the first time she had even been drunk. She was not out joyriding. As a matter of fact, she was picking up her sister. It turned out, as well, that same young woman had lost her mother recently. There she was, working her way through her obligations post-DWI, but her life was deeper than those three letters.

Too many people who get a DWI take it to mean they are unworthy of forgiveness. They make matters worse for themselves, covering up their pain and despair with more alcohol or drugs. Society stereotypes them. Employers won't hire them. Others view them as a threat.

On the other side, there is real hurt to all of this. People lose loved ones to DWIs. In response, they become advocates, like the members of Mothers Against Drunk Driving (MADD). My intention is never to convince them that their pain is unreal or unfounded. No, I just want everyone to look at the world from a wider perspective.

This list is for people on every side of this issue, so everyone can understand the complexities of all this. That said, let's discuss the next ten items.

11. PETS

If your dog or cat is in the car with you while you are driving and you get a DWI, then the police have to take your pet into custody. Your pet will then go into a "pet impound," where he or she will remain for three days. The rules used to say that if, after three days, you failed to retrieve your pet, then the state could euthanize your animal. Yes, by driving while intoxicated, you risked your pet *dying,* and not from a car crash. The rules now state that if you fail to retrieve your pet in the allotted time, then the state will attempt to re-home him or her, allowing others to process an adoption. You will be paying for all of that too.

My advice is not to leave your furry friend at home. On the contrary, anytime you are driving around with your dog or cat, their furry faces should serve as a reminder of your duty to stay sober and drive safely. Pets cannot make the decision themselves to get out of the car and hail a ride home on their own. It is up to you to look out for them, avoiding any situations that would put them in danger needlessly.

In the event that your pet *does* end up in the "pet impound," treat the situation with even more urgency than you would have treated an impounded car. Because of the short, three-day window that you can pick them up, you do not want to waste any time and risk turning your inconvenient circumstances into losing your pet forever.

12. ELDERS

Similarly, if someone who is unable to take care of himself or herself is in the car with you when you get a DWI, then he or she will enter state care. A care provider will look after the elder until you are able to do so. This is not free either. You are going to pay the costs of this care, which could be exorbitant depending on the type of care and attention the elder requires. If you have ever priced out a nursing home or an assisted-living facility, then you know how prohibitively expensive these services can get.

Instead of advice for this list item, I am going to point out the added danger that comes from a DWI with an elder in the car. Elders are at a higher risk of injury, and they are also at a higher risk of mortality, even in less severe crashes. Something like whiplash, which would be a minor injury for a younger person, may be fatal for an elder.

Remember that when you are in the driver's seat. You owe it to all of the people in your car to *think* about the risks you are taking. A DWI is never a sensible risk. When there is an elder involved, however, those risks become even more obvious.

13. CLASSES

My classes, which courts often mandate, are not inexpensive. On top of that, if you are trying to get your license back, you may need to go through a series of courses, fulfilling multiple requirements to make good with the court and to regain your license. These courses will then take up your time; time you could have spent working and earning money for yourself. Whatever the case, you can count on a *huge* dent in your wallet, all to review information you may have heard before.

Considering the expense, the time, and the inconvenience, it would be easy to go into one of these classes with a poor attitude. Trust me when I say that I have seen this *many* times. While a lot of my students show up smiling and ready to learn, others seem unable to get over their own emotions about the situation that brought them to my classroom. I do my best to work with everyone, though I can't help but feel sorry for those who are always looking down, never immersing themselves in the material or opening themselves up to the learning process.

Ideally, you'll never have to attend one of my classes. If you *do* have to attend a class or two, make the most of it by looking on the bright side of things. Show up with a positive mindset and commit to making better choices.

14. AA

At the same time, courts may also mandate Alcoholics Anonymous (AA) meetings. These meetings, although free, are going to eat into your time. Additionally, the transportation you will require to attend in-person meetings will likely not be free. You'll either be paying for an Uber or reimbursing a friend for gas, and that *is* going to cost you. Because AA meetings are ongoing, they will become a regular commitment for you whether or not the meeting day or time is ideal. On Thursdays or Sundays or some other day, when you could have picked up an extra shift at work or spent time with your family, you will be sitting in an AA meeting, working through your challenges as the court has required you to do.

There are *many* resources available to prepare you for your first AA meeting. While no one expects you to arrive understanding all the ins and outs of the program, you will benefit from this type of preparation. Whatever questions are on your mind, try to answer them for yourself before you attend a meeting, so you can dive in and make the most of the group dynamic. AA.org is an excellent place to start.

15. DRUG RECOVERY MEETINGS

Courts may mandate drug recovery meetings instead of or even alongside your required AA meetings. These will also take up hours out of your week, turning into a part of your routine.

If your DWI involves drugs rather than alcohol, then there is no exact path for your recovery. Depending on the specific drugs you have been using, you may choose to or be required to attend a Narcotics Anonymous (NA) meeting or work with a counselor one-on-one. You have to understand what the court expects of you *and* the treatment that will work best for you personally. Again, there are many resources for you to research all of this.

Even better than looking into the resources, though, are the real-world conversations you can have with other people who are recovering or who have recovered from drug abuse. Open up about your struggles and see what you can learn from someone else's journey.

16. REHAB

For especially severe cases of drug abuse and addiction, the court may mandate an extended rehabilitation program. These programs run for weeks at a time and, depending on what the court tells you, you have to either remain in the program indefinitely (until the program director says you have completed it) or serve out a set period of time. Whichever applies to you, you can count on the fact that the bill will be sent to you. These programs are not going to feel good when they hit your bank account.

The cost may not feel good, but if you have spent months or years battling substance abuse, then you know the alternative is *much* worse. During this time, focus on yourself and your own healing. In recent years, people are more often recognizing that addiction is a health issue and not a moral failing. If anyone tries to shame you or embarrass you for getting the healthcare that you need, ignore them. Never let anyone make you feel bad about doing what you need to do to get your life back on track.

17. EQUIPMENT (INTERLOCK, CAMERA, ANKLE BRACELET, SCRAM)

To monitor your behavior and prevent you from getting another DWI, the courts may also require you to wear or install special equipment. Interlock, one of the most popular, is a breathalyzer that you blow into anytime you are getting into your car. It prevents your car from starting unless you are sober. Cameras may track your driving habits and what you are doing while you are at home. Then, there are ankle bracelets, which report your location and your movement throughout the day. Perhaps most restrictive of all, SCRAM is an ankle bracelet that detects alcohol in your blood via a surface liquid test, transmitting its data every thirty minutes.

It should go without saying: whatever the court requires you to install and use in your car, *do not* tamper with it. This is one of the worst things you can do and will turn your difficult situation into an even more challenging one. Put up with the temporary hassle that comes with Interlock, cameras, ankle bracelets, and SCRAM.

Likewise, if you are reading this book because a loved one is going through the post-DWI process, then make sure to remind them to use all of this equipment as directed. You are not helping your friend or family member by showing them ways they may be able to skirt the law.

18. LICENSING

At the end of all your trouble, if the court agrees to reinstate your license, you have to jump through multiple hoops and pay several different fees to secure a new license. This is not as simple as getting your license the first time. Now, you have to convince the court that you are no longer a danger to yourself and to others. The classes, the probation terms, the monitoring equipment data: it is all just building up to an even costlier fee—one that may run into the thousands of dollars—following the processes required to drive again.

I always think of setbacks as opportunities to grow as a person. When I encounter a challenge, and it costs me one thing or another, I ask myself how much better my life can be if I respond to that challenge appropriately.

When you lose your license, it is an opportunity for you to become a better driver and a more responsible citizen. Think of it that way! Instead of going through the motions, take the licensing process seriously. Pay careful attention to all the learning materials and courses that you review, seeing what information may be new to you and what information you may have forgotten from the time since you first got your license.

19. RESTITUTION

Even then, your troubles may not be over. Say you have received a DWI *while* you have caused an accident or damaged someone's property in some way. You have to pay restitution to all of your victims. If one of your victims sues your insurance company, your insurance company may come after you for those funds. It is not uncommon for three or four parties to seek restitution funds from you in the aftermath of a DWI.

There is not much practical upside to paying money to people whose property you have damaged. It is simply something you have to do. If you think about restitution from a more spiritual perspective, it will start to *feel better* for you. Instead of carrying the weight of your mistake indefinitely, restitution provides a means to move on from the damage that you have caused and to do a sort of penance for the people you have wronged.

20. EVALUATION

Someone has to determine whether or not you are capable of continuing to drive. That person, although they hold serious power over you, is also going to charge you for their services. Think about that: you are paying their wages, but by securing this mandatory evaluation, you create more obstacles for yourself. If that sounds like an imbalance of power, it may be, but all you can do is *deal with it*. You are at their mercy.

As you should with every person you encounter during the post-DWI process, cultivate respect. Speak and behave with deference, showing the authorities that you know they are just doing their jobs and that none of this is going to create personal tension between you.

I know it may test your patience to put up with so many people telling you what to do during this period of your life. As a defensive driving instructor, I am often cast in the role of one of these people. Swallow your pride and go along to get along, making the best of your situation.

Reviewing the list thus far, you may notice a pattern: you are looking at major life changes, shifts in the schedule and the responsibilities that you are taking on. All of that is because of one decision you have made: to be intoxicated before you got behind the wheel. Now, we are up to twenty items on our list. It's really heating up now, but let's keep going.

CHAPTER III

One of the youngest men ever to show up in my class was a man who had been high on Xanax. He wrecked his mother's car, totally unaware of what he had done until he woke up in the hospital later. It shocked him to learn that he had been charged with driving under the influence. For him, it was drugs instead of alcohol, but the fires he'd started and penalties accrued were essentially the same.

If you can't put the fires you've started out by yourself—and hopefully you can see by now that in most cases, you can't—by the time everyone else is done putting the flames out for you, the invoice is enormous. Let's keep looking over the items on it.

21. SCHOLARSHIP

For students who get a DWI, scholarships are at stake. Even though the courts can't take away a scholarship directly, they can report the DWI to the college or university that has awarded it. It is then completely legal (and common) for the college or university to revoke the scholarship, leaving you paying a much higher tuition bill. Worse, you may even find yourself locked out of your degree program.

Every day, count your blessings. Someone gave me that advice a long time ago, and ever since I started applying it, I have lived a much happier life. If a scholarship is one of your blessings, reflect on that. The more you acknowledge it, even silently to yourself, the less likely it is that you are going to do anything to risk it.

You owe it to yourself to *protect* all the wonderful things in your present and your future. Embrace them, hold on to them, and try not to do anything that would endanger them and stir up turmoil in your life.

22. FINANCIAL AID

The same rules apply to any need-based financial aid that you have received. Again, it is both legal and common for colleges and universities to revoke this money if you get a DWI. If you look through the terms in the financial aid agreements you have signed, there are clauses that allow the aid administrators to cancel their agreements with you for almost any reason, including misdemeanor and felony convictions.

If you lose financial aid or any other benefit because of a DWI, then it is not going to help you to ruminate on that after the fact. What is done is done. That is not to say that your situation is hopeless. Rather, I recommend that you go looking for *something else*, either another source of financial aid or another opportunity, to replace what you have lost.

A DWI may cause you to feel as if you have backed yourself into a dead end. There is almost always a path forward. Keep yourself open to whatever form of support will replace whatever you have lost.

23. DRIVING RIGHTS

This item may seem straightforward. The costs, however, are not as obvious. Yes, you have to pay to get your driving rights reinstated. You also have to pay for Ubers and Lyfts while you are unable to drive, and if you can no longer afford your commute to work, you may have to take on a lower-paying job—even one that is outside your chosen field.

Sometimes, the growth opportunities that emerge from our mistakes are *not* obvious. They may be subtle. In this case, there is a growth opportunity almost no one is going to recognize. Every time you take an Uber or a Lyft, you can chat up your driver.

Imagine all that you can learn from your driver! Each driver has their own set of life experiences, portions of which they may be willing to share with you. There is a lot you can learn from people, and this represents a great opportunity to soak up some knowledge.

While it would have been better not to get into this situation, if you have to take an Uber or a Lyft everywhere you go, this is one more way you can practice making the most out of your circumstances.

24. NO TAX EDUCATION CREDIT

This is an unexpected cost for many students. The loss of a tax education credit can add up, especially if you have been counting on that credit in your overall tax payment plan.

When losses such as this, as well as scholarship and financial aid losses, begin to mount, you may enlist the help of an advisor, accountant, or other financial professionals to help you. Someone who is well-versed in the financial aspects of education may be able to find *other* forms of financial assistance. Unfortunately, that person will likely also charge for their assistance, but their services can be invaluable for getting your life back on track.

Before you hire someone to guide you through your finances, conduct some research of your own. See what is possible, so that you go into your meeting with some questions. This way, you are getting the most value out of the fees that the professional is going to charge you for their time.

25. PROFESSIONAL LICENSE

Professional licenses, ones that may take you years to earn, are also subject to revocation. Professional counselors, contractors, plumbers, electricians, and teachers may wind up losing entire careers in the event of a DWI. Without the professional licenses that their employers require, they can no longer do the jobs they have trained to do.

My advice for this item is twofold. First, if you *do* lose a professional license, realize that in almost every case, you will be able to get it back at some point. Even though you can't recoup the income you lose during the time you do not hold your license, you can find some comfort in the fact that later on, you will be able to return to the career you have established and make up for the jobs you have missed.

Add to that an awareness that within the job market, you should be able to find *something* temporary. I would recommend that you do so, as soon as possible. Instead of eating into your savings and sitting around mulling over all your stress, keep yourself busy. An idle mind can turn on you, so it's best to do something that either gives back to your community or allows you to put away a few dollars for yourself.

26. COMMERCIAL DRIVER'S LICENSE (CDL)

This is true for truck drivers and delivery drivers too. If you need a CDL to do your job, it may take you months or even years to move past the consequences of your DWI. Every year, otherwise capable commercial drivers have to turn down work and miss out on thousands upon thousands of dollars in earnings, all because they have lost their CDL to a DWI.

Unfortunately, CDLs are some of the most challenging to get back after you have gotten a DWI. Because of the nature of your work, you may encounter red tape that other professionals do not. If you feel discouraged, seek out other CDL holders who have gotten DWIs. This way, you can give yourself some evidence that you are *not* the first professional driver to go through this. They may have industry-specific advice for you to follow as well.

27. COMMERCIAL HANDGUN LICENSE (CHL)

As a convicted felon, if your DWI does turn into a felony charge, you will no longer be able to obtain a CHL. This is an inconvenience for anyone who enjoys owning and firing guns, but for someone who relies on a CHL to do a job (like a police officer or a security guard), it can also mean lost wages or a ruined career.

My advice—and this one would apply to most people who are navigating the post-DWI process—is to take redirection programs seriously. It is always shocking to me to learn that someone who is eligible for a redirection program, such as my course, has turned it down. Whatever hoops you have to jump through to *avoid* a felony conviction, put on your best sneakers and do it!

28. NO CANADA (CRIMINALLY INADMISSIBLE)

Foreign countries are often selective about the people whom they admit over their borders. For Americans who carry the all-powerful "blue passport" this may come as a shock. Americans who have gotten a DWI will run into trouble crossing any border, even the border with our neighbors to the north. Yes, a DWI can render you criminally inadmissible to Canada.

There is not much you can do to bypass international restrictions on felon entry, and even if there were, I would not suggest getting involved in any of that. Instead, my advice is to *accept it* if you have been barred from entering Canada. That may be unfortunate, especially if you have family in Canada, but you do not want to make a bad situation even more dire.

29. CHILD PROTECTIVE SERVICES (CPS)

Most frightening of all to parents are the consequences of a DWI to *children*. If your child is in the car with you when you get a DWI, Child Protective Services will take your child to a foster parent. This is traumatizing for children of any age. It's not just about your child's sudden lack of access to his or her own toys. They will be living with an entirely different family, possibly one with different values than your own, and more importantly, he or she may not understand what is going on.

To get a little bit of motivation to take all of these items seriously, do yourself a favor and look into the foster program. Although staffed by many wonderful people, it is frequently a nightmare for the children who go into it. Fostering would be an extreme outcome in a DWI case, but when CPS steps into the picture, there is no telling how quickly matters can escalate out of control.

30. FAMILY COURT

At the end of your saga with Child Protective Services, you will be paying thousands and thousands of dollars to get your child back into your own custody. More than likely, you will need to retain an attorney, and the process can drag out a *long time*. Family court is there to protect your child, and if the state has taken your child away from you, it means the state is protecting your child from *you*, whether you agree with their assessment or not and whether your child agrees with that assessment or not. The experience of getting your child back may not be an easy or pleasant one.

In family court, as in any court, you are *much* better off hiring an attorney than representing yourself. There is an old saying about the person who represents themselves in court: their clients are *all* fools. As expensive as attorney fees can get, trust that you are paying to prevent outcomes that would be even more expensive and damaging to you and your kids.

You are probably starting to get the picture here: when you are up against a DWI, almost everything is on the table. The courts wield *immense* power, and if they find you guilty, they will use that power to punish you.

CHAPTER IV

Everywhere I go, I meet someone who has experienced one or a number of the things in this book. *That* is how universal DWI challenges are. There are those who have gotten a DWI themselves, as well as those whose friends and family members have gotten a DWI. As little as we talk about these issues in public—and as stigmatized as people who have gotten a DWI *feel*—they are common.

Whether or not you are aware of it, someone in your life has gotten a DWI. It is possible they have kept it a secret from you. If their DWI was severe enough, they will not be able to keep doing that. The consequences of receiving a DWI are so severe and so wide-reaching that they are inescapable. You will start to pick up on hints and clues that something has happened, like unexplained Uber or the repeated court visits. *Something* will give away the secret.

It's already hot in Texas, but a DWI makes it sweltering. Let's keep working our way through the potential consequences.

31. ADULT PROTECTIVE SERVICES

If you are driving with someone sixty-five years of age or older when you get a DWI, you will *not* be able to drive them home with you.

Say you are driving your elderly parent, your grandparent, your aunt, or your uncle: they will have to go to a waiting area in the jail where Adult Protective Services will take him or her into custody. That is *just* as embarrassing and stressful as it sounds, and at the end of it all, you have to pay Adult Protective Services to get your parent, grandparent, aunt, or uncle back.

I want to make it clear that under no circumstances will a police officer make an exception to this rule. If you get a DWI charge while there is someone over the age of sixty-five in your vehicle, you *have* to deal with Adult Protective Services.

I have known some fantastic public servants at Adult Protective Services. Part of what makes them fantastic is they think of older people's needs, not yours. However inconvenient their processes may be for you, it does not matter. Their only concern is ensuring that the elderly person in your vehicle is *safe*. Expect to encounter some (in my opinion, reasonable) hassles as a result!

32. NEWSPAPER

You may have always wondered what it would feel like to see yourself in the newspaper. In your imagination, you may have seen yourself as a hero, smiling on the front page; your name in big, bold letters—something you could clip out and share with your loved ones or include in a scrapbook or hang on your wall. Believe me, that is not how you are going to feel when you see yourself in the police blotter of your local newspaper.

Before I say what I am going to say next, I want to temper your expectations. The odds are *low* that you would ever be able to remove an image or article from a digital archive once it goes online. Few news outlets are even going to respond to such a request.

That said, it *does* happen, and it would not hurt to reach out and make an attempt. Write a letter to the editor of the newspaper or the journalist who has written the article. Explain your situation, politely and clearly, to see if they will show you some mercy and take down your picture at least.

33. MUGSHOT

In addition to appearing in the newspaper, your photo is going to appear on Mugshot.com, where anyone and everyone will be able to download it and share it. Your friends, family, and anyone else who has not already heard about it will find out that you have gotten a DWI. Potential employers will be able to look through this information and can, in most cases legally, choose not to hire you.

One thing you can do, if you fail to get your mugshot taken down from the internet, is build up your online presence. Launch a website and then work on its search engine optimization (SEO), so you are competing with the more negative attention you have gotten. This process is not easy, nor is it cheap. At the same time, there is an ancillary benefit, in that you can use your web presence to promote yourself and develop your career prospects.

Be careful while you are looking for an SEO expert, of course. There are just as many scammers out there as there are qualified advisors! As with most things, you get what you pay for, so this process is not an inexpensive one.

34. FINES

Fines can range from seventy dollars all the way up into *several* thousands of dollars. These costs are likely to mark only the beginning of the burn you'll be feeling in your bank account. At the time, of course, they seem *huge*. You pull a thousand-dollar fine out of its envelope, and you can't help but gasp at it.

The only thing worse than paying a fine is *not* paying it and then racking up interest on it. This is why I would recommend that you pay your fine as soon as you can. You are better off getting it out of the way. Most government agencies will charge you *compounding* interest on missed fine payments. Simultaneously, most of them will also make payment plans available to you, if you happen to need one.

Don't put your fine payment off even a moment longer than you have to!

35. HOUSING

Years after you have gone through the DWI process, you may find yourself trying to get an apartment or a house. You fill out all the forms, knowing that you have saved up enough money for the down payment. It turns out, you are *wrong*. Your landlord runs a background check on you and discovers your DWI, after which it is at your landlord's discretion to allow you to live there or not. You may have to pay a higher deposit than someone else would. This can be three times, four times, five times, or even *six times* more than someone without a DWI would have to pay to live in the exact same apartment or house.

There are a couple of points I can make here. The first is that if you can take higher rent as a sign that it is time to buy, then do so. There are much, much worse outcomes to a DWI than home ownership! Of course, if you cannot afford to buy a home, then I would recommend speaking with your property manager or landlord directly. Explain your situation instead of letting it come up on the background check. If you sense your DWI may be an issue, it can be better to get everything out in the open ahead of time.

36. UBER, LYFT, OR FAMILY AND FRIENDS

In the aftermath of a DWI, you are at other people's mercy to get where you need to go. It is not up to you when you are going to leave somewhere. Instead, you need to match your schedule up to that of your family or friends. Relying on others to take you places is going to become tiresome. As an alternative, you are going to rack up *massive* charges ordering Ubers and Lyfts until you get your license again.

The last thing you want to do is become a burden on the people you care about. If you find yourself leaning on them five, six, seven, or more times per week, it is probably time for you to download Uber or Lyft. Find a balance between these lifelines, using each of them as appropriate and comfortable.

37. NO LOTTERY

After a felony conviction, you become ineligible to participate in the state lottery. That means if you purchase a Mega Millions ticket or a Powerball ticket and hit it big, you have to *relinquish* your winnings. If your DWI leads to a felony conviction, it could wind up costing you *many millions* of dollars, keeping you from the dream life that always seemed so far out of reach to begin with.

Of course, if you have spent too much money on lottery tickets in the past, then this result may not seem all too negative. In that case, I would suggest speaking to a counselor to get to the bottom of your relationship with gambling. While lottery participation may be a fine motivation to keep you from getting your first DWI, hearing this, you may also realize you have not cultivated the healthiest habits in the past.

Throughout this book, or throughout your post-DWI process, consider the mindsets and the attitudes that are driving you. It is *always* worthwhile to ask yourself what you can do better in your life.

38. CREDIT SCORE

Your credit score, following a DWI, is going to go down. If you are someone who has put effort into paying off credit card bills and avoiding risky loans, you are sacrificing years of your life. The car you want, the house you need, all of that will slip through your fingers because a credit score of something like 800 could go all the way to 600 or even lower, depending on other factors.

Credit hits can be painful, particularly if you have put time and effort into building your credit in the past. However, no credit hit is permanent. Bad credit will follow you but not forever. Remind yourself, if you are dealing with a credit drop due to a DWI that on-time payments and responsible finances will push you toward a more desirable situation.

39. WORK OCCUPATION LICENSE

The judge who oversees your DWI case will decide whether or not you can *ever* drive again. If he or she tells you that you can't, then that is the end of the matter. He or she may tell you that you can drive, though, and they may put multiple stipulations on the agreement, which you have to follow to keep your work occupation license. You have to get permission to drive to your job and permission to work certain hours. Once you are working, you have to abide by the rules the judge has set. Failure to do so, or any violation of your work occupation license, could lead to more fees and even an additional arrest.

I am going to reiterate here that when a judge tells you to do something, you *do it*. Their authority, particularly over someone who is going through the post-DWI process, is *immense*. Instead of trying to circumvent any court rulings, play it safe. Whatever you have to do to hold on to your work occupation license, do it, and do it enthusiastically!

40. SR-22

It may seem unfair, but the law is the law. You have to get a special form of insurance called an SR-22, and then keep it inside your car at all times. This SR-22 *will* entail higher fees, something like three times the amount that someone else is paying for standard insurance. Without it, you cannot drive.

For someone who is unfamiliar with the post-DWI process, there is *no reason* to know about SR-22 insurance. As someone who gets a DWI, however, you *have* to know about and understand this financial product. Read up on it, get it, and keep it on your person anytime you are driving.

Let's keep moving along! There is plenty more to cover on our list.

CHAPTER V

When you are in the midst of a DWI situation, you are going to feel as if your whole life will never be the same. You may not have realized how many matches you'd been tossing over your shoulder along the way, but when the officer asks you to get out of your vehicle, you'll have no choice but to confront the wildfire. You will think about all the decisions that have brought you to this point, stretching back for years. However in control you feel, even years down the road, you may feel like you can't help but blame something or someone else. I *get* that. When we are most in pain, the easiest thing is often to push away any self-reflection, to ignore our own actions and choices that have gotten us to where we are.

One young man I spoke to told me that after he got his DUI at the age of seventeen, he couldn't even look at himself. He said that if he looked at himself in a mirror for too long and stared into his own eyes, all of his lies would come crashing down on him. It would feel like he had gotten himself caught up in the truth of the decisions that he had made, and the pain would weigh too heavily on his mind.

It was only after he overcame that type of thinking that he was able to start to heal. That is what I want for you as well. If you have gotten a DWI, or if a family member or a friend of yours has gotten a DWI, I want you to own up to it and face it. I want you to be able to forgive yourself. As difficult as it may be, you need to feel the pain of acceptance before you can feel the joy of *self*-acceptance.

The journey may be long, but it is worth your time and energy. In the meantime, let's take a look at ten more fires we have to put out when we receive a DWI.

41. SOCIAL STIGMA

Depending on the scenario, you will find your name and the details of your DWI splashed across people's computers and cell phone screens. Facebook, Instagram, Twitter, Snapchat, TikTok, and more have all become the public shaming tools of the modern era. Your social media accounts will become burn wards as your peers remind you, subtly or not-so-subtly, of the social stigma attached to your actions. Your family and friends may try to stick up for you at first, but after enough harassment, they will back down. They love you, but they can only do so much. The pain of a stigma like this one can be *horrendous*.

During times like this, when your mental health is most at risk, you are best off talking to a professional. There is nothing wrong with reaching out for help, especially if by doing so, you can avoid even more issues for yourself. Trained, licensed therapists and counselors are available to you. If you feel like the world is against you and the pressure has been too much since your DWI, see what help you can find.

As a start, look into PsychologyToday.com. There, you can look through the therapists in your area, browsing them according to their specialties and reading the short descriptions they provide regarding their services.

42. FAMILY AND FRIENDS

Sadly, less-empathetic family and friends may even join in on the harassment. They will remind you of the social stigma attached to your DWI. At birthday parties, weddings, and other events, they will make sly jokes about your experience, poking fun at you because of what you have gone through. This can be especially, painfully true if alcohol is being served at the event or gathering. If you think you feel embarrassed, just think of how your loved ones feel when they have to hear all of those wisecracks too.

Sometimes the harassment crosses a line, after which there is no turning back. When that happens, you cannot blame yourself. The best thing you can do is to remove yourself from the interaction. However, there are other times when, although the tension is high, communication can make a difference. Start a dialogue with the people in your life, inviting them to share their feelings with you while you listen to them and vice versa.

43. MEDICAL BILLS

If a medical insurer finds out about your DWI, you can count on your premiums and your co-pays to go up, costing you even more. Long term, you are likely to pay hundreds of thousands more than someone who drinks less than you do. On top of that, if your DWI came on the heels of an accident, the costs of your medical treatments may come entirely out of your pocket. This will certainly be true if your insurance company chooses to use your DWI to dispute your coverage.

Healthcare costs can *rapidly* skyrocket out of control. If your debt has become too great for you to manage, you may even have to consider filing for bankruptcy. That should *not* sound like a threat. It is an unfortunate but genuine way out. There is nothing wrong with using the legal system as it is set up. If your DWI puts you in such a precarious situation that it begins to seem there is no coming back from the consequences you are facing, use the options available to you. As I will explain later, a bankruptcy presents lifelong difficulties of its own, but when it is the only option within your reach, you should take advantage of it.

44. ROUTE RESTRICTIONS

If you go to a certain bar all the time, the court may force you to travel a different way to avoid it. That is within their rights. They may dictate *precisely* the route that you have to take to get from your home to your workplace, even if that means you must spend an extra *hour* or two driving every day and pumping extra gallons of gas into your tank every morning. The court will do whatever it must to feel that you are staying safe. Thanks to your DWI, they can make declarations without many limits.

No one likes to spend more time driving than they have to. You may already know what I am going to say, though: you have to make the best of it. Try to enjoy the routes you have to follow in order to avoid the routes that the court has restricted for you. If you've been given a few options, try those different routes. This can help you feel like you are making a decision in the matter.

45. MILITARY

Military service members who have arrived in my class have lost their status and rank as a result of receiving a DWI. In addition, they have seen their pay decrease. The military is very strict about their rules, and they take a very hard stance on any and all DWIs. You *cannot* expect the military to get you out of trouble or to come to your rescue. On the contrary, they will follow up the court's penalties *and* they will add penalties of their own, making your recovery and your rehabilitation even more painful and challenging. So, again, all of this is *in addition to* your consequences as a civilian.

The good news is that in many cases, the military will provide the structure and the discipline you need most as you are navigating the post-DWI process. Whatever care and assistance are available to you, take it. If you can access a counselor because of your military position, you should do that right away. You are, as long as your

DWI does not lead to a court martial, in a fine position to recover from this mistake.

46. GOVERNMENT ASSISTANCE

If you qualify for Medicaid, Medicare, or any other form of government assistance, you may have to forfeit it. Felony status will preclude you from participating in most of those programs, which means you will have to find alternative means to support yourself and supplement your income. As you are, I am sure, realizing by now, those alternative means will be few and far between. You may feel like the government has cut you off in many cases, and you will be right. In this case, they are doing so *literally*. If you're already struggling to find gainful employment because of your DWI, this is one wildfire that could burn on for decades.

As someone who is using government assistance, you may already find it difficult to stay ahead of your financial obligations. Losing that assistance isn't going to help you at all. However, you may learn that there are other, less common forms of assistance, such as grants or even small business loans. Once again, you may be able to turn this difficult period of your life into an opportunity if you research and learn enough about what is within your reach.

47. BACKGROUND CHECKS

Make no mistake about it: a DWI *stays* on your record. It *will* come up on background checks, whether you are trying to get a job or trying to secure a mortgage. Anytime a police officer runs your plate or your driver's license in the system, your DWI is going to pop up. It is permanent and inevitable. A background check will also reveal your DWI to anyone looking, causing you all sorts of issues down the line. The only thing you can do to avoid setting this particularly permanent wildfire is to avoid getting a DWI in the first place.

I am not going to leave you there, though. Even though the most attractive employers will require you to go through a background check, they may make exceptions with regards to their rules and their findings, if you have presented yourself well enough.

Knowing that a DWI is going to come up on your background check, you should put forth *that much more effort* during the application and interview stages. Make it clear that if you get the job, you are going to become a role model for all the other employees at the organization.

48. DIVORCE

She's tired. She's fed up. Now, she wants to get a divorce. The relationship that meant the most to you is now a smoldering pile of ashes; nothing like the thing it was before your DWI set it on fire. You are losing the love of your life because of your DWI. Divorce is life-changing and difficult. Some people take to drinking even more, seeking solace at the bottom of a bottle of whiskey, while others pick up the pieces and go looking for a new spouse. Whichever way you go, it is not going to be easy. To protect yourself and your assets, you may have to hire an attorney to help you navigate through the mess. While it is possible to represent yourself, you'll wish you had an attorney present when your ex tells the judge all about your DWI and why they should receive more than you think they should because of *your* struggles.

This advice is suitable for *anyone* who is getting a divorce, but particularly for anyone who is getting a divorce because of a DWI. When you communicate with your attorney, when you are in court or arbitration, and in any texts or phone calls with your soon-to-be ex, keep your cool. Remain calm, avoiding any unseemly outbursts. You are not helping yourself by shouting, even if you feel like your perspective is going unheard.

49. CHILD SUPPORT

She *will* be hitting you up for child support. And ladies, if you're the one who receives the DWI, you can count on *him* hitting you up for child support as well. One woman I knew lost custody of her children to her husband because she was drinking so much. It happened after she went bar hopping, drove under the influence, hit someone, blew a 0.08% BAC (blood alcohol content), and went to jail. After that, she didn't see her own children for *years*, all because of one night that went as badly as any night could go.

Anytime there are children in the scenario, you have to think of them and their needs above all else. Ask yourself what is right for them, not just what you can afford to pay. While you are going to present your case in front of the judge either way, remind yourself that child support *should* benefit the young people who are most important to you. That should provide some solace!

50. CUSTODY BATTLES

Sometimes, however, the situation is even messier. One father had to fight his own parents for custody of his children. They sued after he got his DWI, and because he was then a felon, the court heard the case. He barely retained custody of his son and daughter. That was a difficult experience for the entire family, and by the time it was over, he had paid thousands upon thousands of dollars in court and attorney fees.

It is difficult to see the bright side of a situation in which your family is getting broken up. Instead of asking you to do that, I would suggest that you hire the best attorney you can find. You want someone who is going to go to bat for you—a true fighter who will show up for you and represent your interests effectively.

During *every* step of the post-DWI process, I want you to resist the urge to blame others. In the end, we are responsible for our choices and actions. Acceptance of this is a positive first step in getting your life back on track after a DWI.

DWIs happen to people from all walks of life. In November 2021, Henry Ruggs III had the world at his fingertips. He had been a standout on the Alabama Crimson Tide football team, playing a key role in the team winning a national championship in 2017. When he declared for the NFL draft in 2020, it was clear that he was one of the most desirable wide receivers in the league. The Las Vegas Raiders selected him with the twelfth pick in the first round.

That season, Henry Ruggs made an immediate impact. In a draft class filled with duds, Ruggs was putting in the work and putting up the numbers. He garnered league-wide acclaim for his talent and his maturity. Even better, trends throughout the NFL meant that wide receivers were winning bigger and bigger contracts. Ruggs would be in line for a payday as soon as his rookie contract was up. In the meantime, he was living the high life, earning millions of dollars per year and starring on one of the most popular sports teams in the world.

In November 2021, while driving his sports car through Las Vegas, he blew through a red light and slammed into a car that was turning out of a parking lot. The crash ejected Ruggs from his seat and through his windshield. It also caused the car that he hit to explode. The driver of the car, twenty-three-year-old local Las Vegan Tina Tintor, did not die instantly. Instead, she burned to death, while Ruggs and his girlfriend sat by the side of the road, unable to help, forced to watch as both Tintor and Ruggs's dreams of NFL stardom went up in flames.

Tina Tintor had come from an immigrant family. Sitting beside her in her car was her dog, who also died in the fire. In the hour that followed, it became clear that Ruggs had been driving drunk. His speed, according to surveillance cameras in the area, had exceeded

156 miles per hour. Afterward, Ruggs's girlfriend needed to undergo surgery due to her injuries from the crash.

At the time of this writing, Ruggs is still going through court proceedings. Only twenty-two years old, he is looking at somewhere between two and fifty years in prison if he is convicted of the felonies he has been charged with.

CHAPTER VI

Sometimes deaths in the news roll right off your shoulders. There is so much suffering in the world that we have become desensitized to it. Certain stories change that though. They are too painful to ignore, particularly when they happen close to your home.

When I read about Allie White's death in 2019, I couldn't ignore it at all. It stuck with me that day, and it remained with me thereafter.

Allie White was two years old when she died in Round Rock, Texas, not far from where I live. She was enjoying a Sunday at the park with her family, while her sister played soccer on a nearby field. A car struck the toddler, and, like Tina Tintor, the accident did *not* lead to an immediate death. Instead, the front tire picked up the toddler, rolling her around, until she hit the ground, and then the back tire did the same thing. Lodged under that back tire, Allie White passed away before her mother could reach her.

There was, unlike the Ruggs's case, no alcohol involved. Instead, the driver had been distracted. Although she claimed afterward that she was not using her phone and was only holding it in her hand, the outcome was the same: an innocent life had been taken.

This story is horrific, as so many of these stories are. I know they must be hard for you to read. They are hard for me to *write*. We need to keep these stories in mind though. Unless we remind ourselves of these consequences, the Allie Whites and the Tina Tintors of the world will have died in vain. We need to learn from these experiences so we don't repeat them.

Let's keep moving with the list.

51. IMMIGRATION

If you're an immigrant who gets a DWI, you have to get an immigration lawyer. The government may, depending on the situation, try to force you to go back to your country. They may revoke your visa, your green card, or your work permit. All of those are possible issues for immigrants. It may happen in a week, but this could also take a month. The government does not need to stick to any timeline when they are considering or reconsidering your privileges as an immigrant. A DWI may be all the reason they need to make your life *extremely* complicated.

During immigration proceedings, one of the most impactful things you can do to help yourself is to collect recommendation letters from people in your community. Ask your friends, family members, and associates to write about you. Explain to them beforehand what this letter would mean to you and what it may do for you, as you are facing one of the most difficult times in your life.

On top of that, you need to make sure you are on excellent terms with your employer and that no one who holds any of your debt is going to become upset for any reason. You do not want to give an immigration court any other reason to look unkindly on your docket.

52. DEPORTATION

Consequences for immigrants may run all the way up to deportation. If you are in the United States on a green card or some other type of work visa, then the federal government *will* receive a notification that you have gotten a DWI. In most cases, they will take action in some way, either forcing you to pay additional fees to keep your green card or work visa or sending you back to your home country. At that point, it is unlikely you will ever be allowed back into the United States.

When families get broken up, it causes turmoil for multiple generations. This is *always* a tragedy. You can alleviate the effects of deportation through clear and constant communication with everyone in your life. Come up with a plan together. It can be terrifying and traumatizing if ICE agents show up in the middle of the night to remove you from your home.

53. CITIZENSHIP

Many of these rules also apply to immigrants who are going through the citizenship process. Until you have *gained* citizenship status, nothing is off the table. I heard from one young man who, after years of lawful living in this country and only a month away from his citizenship exam, had to return to his home in South America. He had earned his college degree in the United States with good grades, and he was working a high-paying job. In an instant, his DWI burned down all of his accomplishments and made them irrelevant in the US government's perspective.

Unfortunately, for someone who is working toward citizenship, a DWI almost always puts an end to the process. My advice is to adjust your goals and expectations. Instead of getting hung up on citizenship and what it would mean for you and your family, figure out if you can get an extended work permit so you can at least remain in the country.

54. VISA

No visa is immune to the consequences of a DWI. Student visas, special exchange visas, and even tourism visas are all subject to revocation for anyone who gets a DWI. The government tends to move quickly on these issues, taking much less time to revoke visas than they do to grant and distribute them. Ask anyone who has ever lost a visa: they are all but impossible to regain once they're lost.

Again, I am not going to lie to you and tell you there is some secret method to get out of this mess. When the federal government finds out about a DWI, they often act swiftly and exercise little to no forgiveness. My best advice in this situation is to remain calm and to foster some degree of confidence that, in time, you will find other opportunities to set your life right.

55. GREEN CARD

If you rely on a green card to stay in the United States and earn a living, a DWI may put an end to it. If you read the fine print on your green card, it mentions your green card is subject to revocation at any time and for *nearly any reason*. A DWI—especially if the DWI is a felony—certainly falls into that category. You may find that you can no longer reside in the United States if you get a DWI, let alone find gainful, legal employment while you are here.

Fortunately, the online gig economy has opened up new opportunities outside the purview of local employment regulations. If you are unable to secure a green card but you can still remain in the United States for other reasons, you may look into remote work. There are many opportunities at call centers that employ people from around the world. All you need to get started is a headset, a computer, and an internet connection.

56. WORK PERMIT

A work permit is even more restrictive. Therefore, like the green card, this means you are even more likely to lose it if you get a DWI. Upon revoking your work permit, representatives of the United

States government will show up at your home or place of business to take you into custody and deport you.

It is important to note: *there is no time limit on this*. They could decide to revoke your permit as soon as you get your DWI charge or as late as your conviction.

While you are navigating the post-DWI process, prepare for your situation to degrade rapidly. There is no telling when the government will decide to revoke your work permit. If that happens, you should be able to fall back into a secondary plan. You *don't* want to set yourself up for a situation in which you feel you have no options. That is only going to make your stress worse and exacerbate all of the issues you are already handling.

57. DEMOTION

For anyone who gets a DWI and who works, citizen or not, an official or unofficial demotion may be burning bright on the horizon. Say you're making fifty thousand dollars a year. As you've surely gathered by reading thus far, complications from a DWI could cut your salary in half or even drag it down to zero. You may very well lose the job you've been working to support yourself. Without a job, you can't do any of the things that have become habits for you and, if you have a family, you will struggle to find a way to meaningfully contribute. You may need to cut back on your budget in all areas, even housing and food. Because of background checks, you may have to settle for a less-than-ideal job. You can be sure your DWI has the potential to make it very difficult for you to ever move out of your new, lower-paying position.

Remember that although bosses and managers still have to answer to *their* bosses and managers, people are still people. If you go in to talk to someone and explain your circumstances, they may be willing to listen. While they may *not* be, you never know unless you try. Overcome any anxiety you are feeling and strike up a conversation with the decision makers who hold the keys to your future.

58. NO GIRL/BOY SCOUT LEADERSHIP

This is one of the consequences that few people would ever consider and usually don't until they run into it headfirst. Both the Boy Scouts and the Girl Scouts run background checks on all their leaders. If your child chooses to join the Boy Scouts or the Girl Scouts, you will not be able to participate. The opportunity to make memories with your child and all of the mentoring you could have provided disappears, catching fire before your eyes. You will find yourself left out in the cold, isolated from the social situation that is now a dominant force in your child's life.

This one was a surprise to me when I first heard about it in my class! It is, like so many aspects of the post-DWI process, something you would never consider until it became a problem for you. If you believe a background check is going to be a problem for you (and your children are not already in the Boy Scouts or Girl Scouts), consider steering your children toward different activities where you are still a welcome participant.

59. URINALYSIS

Every time you meet with your probation officer or your parole officer, you have to provide a urine sample so they can test it and make sure you are neither taking drugs nor drinking excessive alcohol. If your urinalysis comes back positive, that is another set of problems, but even if your urinalysis comes back negative, you are responsible for payment. You have to cover all the costs associated with the urinalysis, which can run into the *hundreds* of dollars because your health insurance is not going to cover it.

Don't try to cheat on a urine test. Many have tried. Some have succeeded, but far more have failed. Despite all the instructions available on the internet explaining in detail how you can sneak fake or clean urine into the testing center, it is not worth the risk. Stop drinking and stop taking drugs so you can pass the urinalysis on your own. If necessary, speak to a counselor who can help you break your addiction.

60. HEALTH INSURANCE

On the subject of health insurance, your premium is certain to go up because of your DWI. You have to pay that premium or pay the penalty associated with foregoing health insurance. Some people will opt for lower-quality, lower-priced health insurance, while others will pay the higher premiums, taking a chunk out of their own savings. The latter may not be a bad idea because, as we will discuss soon, there are some *deadly* health challenges on the horizon for many of the heaviest drinkers out there.

I suggest shopping around, even if it seems that none of the insurers are going to cut you a better deal. Students have told me about unconventional approaches; some of them even hop from agent to agent to get a better deal on their health insurance. These costs add up, which means they are worth examining and researching closely.

Few people who knew Jacqueline Saburido would have recognized her by the time she was a public figure. However, after a crash set her on fire and left her severely disfigured, she found her voice and became an advocate for others who were or who would be in the same situation.

It was September of 1999. Saburido and her friends were driving home from a birthday party, traveling on roads that were familiar around Austin, Texas. Not long after they left the event, Reginald

Stephey's GMC Yukon slammed into Saburido's Oldsmobile. The car caught fire, and one of Saburido's friends died at the scene. Saburido's two surviving friends escaped the burning vehicle. Unfortunately, Saburido remained stuck inside. First responders arrived at the scene quickly, but not quickly enough to prevent the fire from spreading to Saburido's body. To make matters worse, the fire *started again* while first responders were attempting to get the Oldsmobile door open and pull Saburido to safety. For more than a minute, flames covered Saburido's entire body.

At the burn unit in Galveston, Texas, doctors who specialized in Saburido's types of injuries performed multiple surgeries to ensure her survival. At the time, few experts thought she would live. She overcame the odds, though second- and third-degree burns had cost her all of her fingers, her nose, her hair, her ears, one of her eyelids, and her lips. Saburido lived to talk about her experience, and she endured more than 120 surgeries in the years that followed.

Saburido applied for a face transplant, which was groundbreaking at the time, but researchers did not select her. When she was denied that help, she endured a cornea transplant to recover some of the vision she had lost.

Eighteen months after the crash, the man behind the wheel of the car who struck her, Reginald Stephey, stood trial. Saburido was there at the trial, speaking in public for the first time about the chaos that Stephey's DWI had caused her. She said, "[Stephey] destroyed my life." However, in an act of grace, she expressed her forgiveness for the driver. After his sentencing, Stephey commented that when Saburido said she forgave him, it changed his life. Her forgiveness, despite all the turmoil his poor decision-making brought about, was the first positive thing to come out of that crash, but not the last.

Saburido could have tried to hide from the world, obscuring her injuries out of shame or embarrassment, but she didn't. Instead, she went to major media outlets and encouraged them to publish the photos of her injuries. Multiple newspapers and TV networks spread her photos to their audiences, using Saburido as an example of the *horror* that drunk driving could wreak.

For several years, Saburido embraced the role of poster child for the anti-drunk-driving movement. The internet, which was still in its infancy, became host to videos and emails featuring her and her injuries. During one commercial, funded by an advocacy group, she posed next to a photo of herself taken before the crash.

Of her advocacy work, Saburido said, "I feel very good to do it because I know people can understand a little more what happened to me and why my life changed completely. So I think for me, for everybody, it's a good opportunity." She made appearances throughout Texas schools, working with mental health professionals to come up with positive, effective messaging that teachers and administrators could show to children without traumatizing them.

Saburido was a constant presence in public life for almost twenty years after the crash. She appeared on some of the largest shows on television, including *The Oprah Winfrey Show*, making herself available to anyone who wanted to discuss the realities of her situation. Doing nothing to deserve her fate, she nonetheless accepted it, and she turned it into something that would change people's hearts and minds for the better.

CHAPTER VII

You may find yourself seeking comfort in the idea that even though the court system and DWI process are difficult, at least it's fair. You may find yourself thinking that everyone else has to go through the same scrutiny and trouble as you.

That would be a nice, reassuring thing to hear or believe, but it's not the truth.

The truth is that the court system often treats some people better than it treats other people. In one famous case, a judge determined that a young man had caught a case of *affluenza,* something the judge appeared to find pitiable. That is to say, after the young man drove drunk, injuring nine people and killing four, he only ever served two years in prison (and on an entirely different charge). As of 2021, he was released back into the world, free to do as he pleased.

Unless your parents can spend the money that young man's parents spent on his defense, judges are unlikely to look upon your DWI case quite as kindly. In fact, if you *try* to make excuses to get out of a charge, they may choose to throw the book at you, upgrading your misdemeanor to a felony or sentencing you beyond the time that the prosecutors have recommended.

That is our society, for better and for worse. Judges operate with a wide range of discretion, choosing how to punish the defendants who appear in their courtrooms. It is *not* worth taking the risk to hope that you will get off as easily as the *affluenza* man did. Show up to court and plead "affluenza" and the judge will, in her own way, hand you a tiny bucket and instruct you to put out a ten-mile-wide wildfire.

61. CAR DAMAGE

Any car damage you cause during the event that earned you your DWI becomes your *sole* responsibility. This rule applies not only to the damage you cause to your own car but to the damage you cause to any other car as well. If your insurance company declines to cover you, then you must pay all those damages out of pocket. Either way, you have to make everyone you affect *whole*. This means paying whatever it takes to smother the flames you and your DWI caused.

As a side note, I would recommend taking *extreme* care anytime you hire an auto mechanic for extensive repairs. It is always a great idea to get multiple opinions about any work you need done on your vehicle. Ask for at least three different opinions, especially if your insurance provider will not be paying for any of the damages.

62. PRE-TRIAL DWI PROGRAMS

Sometimes you *may* get lucky: that is what a pre-trial DWI program represents. It is a stroke of good luck that can keep that DWI off your record, so it does not show up on a normal background check. Still, there is the time and the expense to consider. You may be able to avoid a plea, but to get to that point, you have to work. The court wants to know you are serious about avoiding any DWIs in the future and that you have learned your lesson. In addition, the charge will *still* show up in police records, which makes it relevant during any traffic stops you encounter in the future.

When you have entered a pre-trial DWI program, the best course of action is to treat it as a fresh start. This is a time for you to reflect on all the habits that have led you to this point and to make all the changes you need to make. You will likely realize that some of the things you have done in the past *seemed* harmless but put you into situations where the temptation to make a bad decision was irresistible.

Look inward throughout the post-DWI process. A counselor, a pastor, a former teacher, a mentor, and an elder will each provide you with different and valuable advice. Open your heart to them and take whatever you can from their words.

63. MINOR CONSUMPTION

If you are under the age of twenty-one, like the young man the judge said caught *affluenza*, then your DWI is a *DUI*. The "minor consumption" laws apply to you. These are *not* free passes. If you plead guilty to a DUI, you are subject to almost all of the same penalties that would fall upon someone who gets a DWI. The only difference is that the judge is more likely to consider your eligibility for pre-trial programs to avoid jail time and a criminal record.

Many minors who have gone through my classes have come out *the best* afterward. This runs contrary to what's commonly believed. A lot of people, even the minors' own parents, believe that a DUI spells the end of any young person's future. Nothing could be further from the truth.

As a minor, you *can* put your life back on course. Focus on the things that matter most, such as your academics and any sports you play, to compensate for the extra stress you have to handle. The more you concentrate on activities that will enable you to grow as a person, the more quickly you can put this period of your life behind you.

64. PASSPORT REVOCATION

When you get a DWI, the State Department may revoke your passport. To get it reinstated, you have to pay whatever charges and fees they put in front of you. Even then, you may not be able to get travel visas for all the countries you want to visit.

Say that you are *never* able to travel to some of the far-off locations you have dreamed about visiting. A DWI is crushing in that regard, preventing you from seeing Notre Dame in Paris and the Vatican in Rome. While there is no substitute for visiting those places yourself, the internet has made it possible for you to *come close* to experiencing them from the comfort of your home.

If you realize that your DWI precludes you from international travel, think of ways that you can immerse yourself in your dream destinations anyway. Watch videos and read articles created by those who have traveled to those places, not to torture yourself, but to show yourself that your life has not ended just because of your DWI. There are still *plenty* of experiences ahead of you.

65. LOG BOOK

Your log book, which assures the court that you are not going anywhere they have not permitted you to go, stays in your car at all times. You have to make a record of everything you do and log every stop. If the police stop you, they have to check if you're going where you're allowed to go. This is annoying to fill out, but even more than that, it may feel embarrassing and constraining, as if someone is always breathing down your neck and telling you what you can and cannot do.

Accuracy is key in your log book. When you write something down in it, read over it twice to ensure you are not missing anything. You want to create clear and precise records for the court. A judge who sees that you have put effort into your log book is *much* likelier to look kindly upon you throughout the remainder of the post-DWI process. The worst thing you can do is leave out a crucial detail and only notice it when the judge points it out to you.

66. BANKRUPTCY

It is not uncommon for someone who has gotten to the end of the DWI process to find that they have wiped out all of their savings. Sometimes they will even take out second mortgages or pawn their most precious belongings. Then they have to file for bankruptcy. These protections make it possible for them to restructure and renegotiate their debt. Unfortunately, for the most part, those who file for bankruptcy will never get back to their former financial status. They will struggle for years on end just to get by, saving nothing and barely staying fed.

After you have filed for bankruptcy, seek out proper, professional advice. Talk to a financial advisor to plan out your next steps. Most of the time, if you hold a retirement account or a qualified savings account through a bank or insurer, they will connect you with a financial advisor free of charge. Note that financial advisors generally *do not* charge you fees for their services. Instead, they will consult with you for free, in the hopes that you will choose them to manage your money when you set up additional investments.

67. TAXES

Although uncommon, higher or special taxes for those who have gotten a DWI *do* exist. The IRS will come looking for those taxes as well, as they will consider them part of your overall debt to the government. When that happens, there is no way around it. You may even be a year, two years, or three years *past* your DWI conviction. The government doesn't care; they are going to get their money.

They intend to claim and collect whatever they've determined you owe, even if they have to garnish your wages to get it.

There are few organizations in history as powerful as the IRS. When Al Capone finally got busted during the Prohibition Era, it was *his taxes* that did him in. It would be a dangerous error of judgment to think you can ignore any higher or special taxes and fines that the IRS levies against you.

Whenever you receive a letter from the IRS during the post-DWI process, bump it up to the top of your to-do list. Figure out what they want from you and how you can fulfill your obligations as quickly as possible.

68. JUDGMENTS/LIENS

To avoid bankruptcy, you may take out a reverse mortgage or a second loan against a car or some other valuable piece of property. That seems fine while you are doing it, but when you have to pay for that loan and can't, your lender can file for a *lien* against your property. Judgments and liens are commonplace in DWI cases because bankruptcies are so frequent. Unless you file for bankruptcy protection and renegotiate what you owe, you *have* to pay them.

Reverse mortgages should *always* be your last resort. If you are eligible for any type of loan, or if there is anyone you can ask for help, that option would be preferable to a reverse mortgage. In most cases, reverse mortgages are suitable only for our elders who are trying to put together the last bits of money they need to live out their retirement.

Before you sign on to a reverse mortgage, look elsewhere. I recommend it here only so you know it is an option for you, but I do not recommend it in any way. The contracts that go along with reverse mortgages are notoriously predatory. Avoid them if at all possible.

69. CIRRHOSIS OF THE LIVER

Remember what we said about health insurance on this list. After a DWI, it gets *pricey*. To make matters worse, cirrhosis of the liver—which leads to liver failure—is common among those who drink too much. If you are at the point that you are getting a DWI, cirrhosis may not be far off. In ten or twenty years, you will realize your DWI was among the first signals that you should have slowed down.

Your DWI may not be enough to wake you up from the haze that you are in because of your alcohol consumption. In that case, do some research into cirrhosis of the liver. Look at photos of cirrhosis patients and realize that if you neither slow down nor cut out alcohol consumption, their fate may soon be your own.

Even though a DWI is enough of a signal for some people, others require more. That is *fine*. My suggestion is to go *looking* for more information and education. Don't wait for catastrophe to come looking for you.

70. TERM AND WHOLE LIFE INSURANCE

There is nothing prohibiting life insurance companies from charging you higher rates for term and whole life insurance policies. In fact, they work those variables into all of their calculations. When you apply for a life insurance policy, either as a form of savings or as a tool to protect your loved ones, you can expect to pay a much higher premium than you would have paid if you had never gotten a DWI.

None of this is to say that life insurance is an unwise investment, especially if you are investing for your loved ones as well as for yourself. Sometimes in spite of the higher premiums, whole life insurance is *still* worth whatever it costs you. Consult a financial professional as well as someone you trust to see what life insurance is worth to you, both in monetary terms and for your own peace of mind.

There is, after all, nothing that will stay with you like knowing you have hurt or let down someone you should have protected. Carl Keating learned that lesson the hard way. At thirty-two years old, he was driving under the influence of marijuana when, court records say, he challenged another car to a race on a Pennsylvania road.

Keating's girlfriend, Rebecca Koorsen, was in the passenger seat that day. Speeding and impaired, he crashed the car, killing Koorsen. Police officers tested his blood, which returned a positive result for marijuana. This story gets to the core of something I hear all the time in my classes. Unfortunately, people do *not* take marijuana as seriously as they do other substances. This can be a costly and deadly mistake.

If you are driving while you are under the influence of marijuana, you *can* get a DWI. If you cause a death, as Keating did, you will face the same penalties as someone who had been under the influence of alcohol or prescription drugs. All of this pales in comparison, of course, with the real-world cost: Koorsen was only twenty-eight years old when she died. In the aftermath of the crash, it did not matter that Keating thought marijuana was "less serious" than other drugs.

It only mattered that he chose to drive while he was impaired.

At his trial, Keating spoke about the grief that he experienced since the crash. He said, "It haunts me every day. When I close my eyes at night, it's all I see."

CHAPTER VIII

Not too long ago, a woman came into my class in support of her son, and she told me a story about what he had gone through. He had been so high on narcotics while driving that by the time the cops arrested him, he didn't know where he was. He was unresponsive to their questions, and what little he did say made no sense. In the aftermath, he faced multiple charges, including a DWI. His life would never be the same, but when asked what happened afterward, he had little to offer in the way of answers—he couldn't even remember what substances he had taken.

While blacked out, that young man also walked into someone else's house, stole their property, ran into someone's garage, drove over and destroyed multiple mailboxes, and hit a pedestrian. He damaged both private and public property, racking up well over six figures in damages, all of which his mother had to pay.

Take all of that in. When that mother and her son woke up, neither of them said that they wanted to ruin any lives or cause any damage. Neither of them decided that they were going to crash into a garage or steal someone's property. In the young man's case, he might never have *known* he was driving, at least not consciously. Even so, he (and his generous mother) paid the price, all the same.

He was responsible for the damage that he caused. We all are, and that is always the case—affluenza defense aside. When someone gets a DWI and causes damages, they have to pay to make up for it. Either we must put out our fires ourselves or the state will involve others who will do it for us, like lawyers and parole officers. Think of them as the "firefighters" in your DWI wildfire scenario. These people are mandatory, and they are often assigned to you or your case whether you like it or not.

71. SPOUSAL SUPPORT

If your spouse has come to rely on you for an income, they will sue you for spousal support. These payments, as frustrating as they would have been in any situation, will become overwhelming when you add them to all the other payments you are making on fines, restitution, probation, and rehabilitation. Someone who wants little or nothing to do with you will get a piece of your paycheck for a painful period of time, because the judge ruled that your DWI was a reasonable cause for a divorce.

As with child support, the worst thing you can do here is lose your temper. Throughout spousal support proceedings and in all communications, try to keep an even keel. Keep in mind that you are responsible for protecting your own interests and that courtroom outbursts are *not* going to do that. I have heard from many students who have created more problems for themselves by shouting at judges or attorneys. As the defendant in a lawsuit, you are never going to get yourself anywhere by lashing out because things seem unfair to you.

72. ALIMONY

Alimony is a strong possibility of any divorce. If your husband or your wife no longer wants to be with you, then you may have to provide payments after you split. Like spousal support, because of your DWI, the odds that a judge will grant your ex-spouse alimony will increase. Your DWI shows up like three scarlet letters on your court filings, which is evidence that your partner is justified in asking to dissolve your marriage agreement.

At the very least, prepare a strong defense for your DWIs. This does *not* mean you are attempting to explain away or justify your DWIs. Rather, it means that you are outlining the ways that you have moved forward from your DWI, putting the conviction into its context so that the judge can see you as a real person.

One of the most difficult tasks in the world is to talk about yourself. If you feel like it is *too* difficult for you to explain the work you have done to move on from your DWI, hire an attorney or paralegal to help you. They can put your thoughts in order so that when your court date arrives, you are not stumbling over your words.

73. SUPPORT GROUP

Another stipulation the judge may include in his filing against you is attendance at a support group. The judge may order this in addition to or in conjunction with AA. You must attend these meetings week after week, month after month, perhaps for multiple years. The idea is that your support group will guide you away from any temptations, helping you to stop drinking or to cut back enough to avoid a DWI. This can be helpful for some, but few people like being forced to do anything, including seeking help. Of course, you will also be required to pay whatever fees the support group charges you.

Still, there is *no replacement* for grace, which is what you will get in a support group. Hearing from people who are in situations similar to yours, you will understand that despite all that has gone wrong in your life, you are not alone. On top of that, it may be easier for you to admire and respect the other people in your support group than it is for you to admire and respect yourself. In turn, you will be able to see more clearly that this single mistake does not define you.

Even if it's not ordered by a judge, a support group is a gift you can give yourself when you are hurting and down on your luck!

74. WEEKEND

If you are like most people, then you probably look forward to the weekend from the moment you arrive at work on Monday. If you're on work release as part of a DWI rehabilitation program, your weekend *goes away*. The judge may say that since you're working, you can report to jail on the weekend, and you'll have to stay in jail Friday through Sunday. None of your old activities are possible anymore. Any weekend leagues, any weekend dates, and most social events will be out of bounds for you.

I cannot stress enough that as little time as there will be for the "fun things" in life, you still have to figure out a balance for yourself. When you can't do what you would like to do in your free time, all of your stress will begin to weigh that much more heavily on you. To avoid burnout or a breakdown, come up with a plan to relax and unwind, shaking off your stress as a ritual, even if that ritual looks nothing like your old lifestyle.

75. ID ONLY

If your driver's license has been revoked, you have to get an ID to do all the things that you would otherwise need a driver's license for, like to prove your age or identity. In some places, the difference will create confusion. People will look at your ID and fuss over it, drawing attention to the fact that you don't have a regular license. This may feel humiliating. IDs do, after all, invite speculation as to *why* you do not have your driver's license.

If you speak with a therapist or a pastor, they will tell you the same things about humiliation, shame, and embarrassment. These are powerful emotions, but they are emotions nonetheless; things that you can understand and overcome through faith and the proper mindsets. When you feel your cheeks turning red or you can't help but get down on yourself, ask yourself what you would say to a friend who felt the same way. Then, say that very thing to yourself.

Give *yourself* the gift of friendship when you are handling something like an ID restriction. Instead of imagining that everyone who sees the ID is judging you, realize that people are going through their own difficulties and paying little mind to yours anyway. Even if they *do* notice, their judgments do not define who you are as a person.

76. PUBLIC DAMAGES

Anything considered "public property" will entail a huge amount of money. If you break it or damage it, you have to pay whatever the contractors are going to charge the taxpayers. By and large, government contracts cost more than commercial contracts do. For example, if you break a public rail, the cost starts at $5,000 and only goes up. For trees and buildings? It's the same thing. There is no tree more expensive than a public tree, as you will discover when they send you the bill. The number at the top of that invoice will all but burn your eyes. You can be sure all the extra money is coming directly out of your bank account.

As a rule, you should pay close attention to your finances during the post-DWI process. Keep your own records of the money that is coming in and the money that is going out. Although government agencies are careful for the most part about any debits they make, it is up to you to verify that no one is overcharging you for anything.

Anytime you are unsure about an amount of money you are paying for public damages, it is your right to check in. Pick up the phone, explain your situation, and confirm that you are not paying any more than you should be paying.

77. PRIVATE DAMAGES

Do not downplay damages to private property. If you break or harm *anything*, you are responsible for it. Other cars, people's homes, and people's belongings all cost money. Whether someone files an insurance claim or sues you outright, they are going to get the value of their property *back*. Private damages—don't confuse this—can run into the tens and hundreds of thousands of dollars, the same way public damages can.

Even though everyday citizens may not be able to push back the way that the government can, you are still best off responding to inquiries and letters as you receive them. Often, you are relying on other people's goodwill when you are navigating the post-DWI process. You may not realize until it is too late that if you upset someone, they are going to make your life a lot more difficult.

Of course, if you disagree with any of the charges or complaints that someone files about you, then you can challenge them in court. There is a difference between treating people with respect and acquiescing to every request that they make.

78. TRUST

Less tangible but no less real, trust in you may fade if you get a DWI. For example, if your DWI has lost you the trust of your peers, you will notice they doubt you when you tell them you are going to do something. The respect and deference they would have shown you otherwise? You lose that as well. Your friends and family members may view you as unreliable and irresponsible because of the mistake you have made.

Trust is something you earn over time. In the months after your

DWI, try not to worry too much about the trust that you have lost or the relationships you have changed. While you are rectifying your circumstances from the damage that your DWI has caused, you should devote all your energy and attention to specific, practical concerns.

Pay your fines, work with the courts, and get your life on track. Once you have finished those tasks, you can spend more of your time repairing your connections with your peers and showing them they can trust you again.

79. IN THE SYSTEM

A DWI means you are "in the system." This means the FBI system and the local system alike. Anytime a police officer pulls you over, they see your stops and your DWI(s). Police can see that with a single click. As soon as the police have pulled you over and charged you for a DWI, they can track you on their computers, looking into your past and then creating a record of your arrest. Every time you go out driving from then on, they can see you just by pulling up your license plate number in their comprehensive database.

One piece of advice I wish I did not have to offer, but know from experience that I do, is: do *not* lie to the police during a traffic stop. Even a lie that seems tiny may upset police officers and put them on edge. Any questions the police ask you about your past, you should answer truthfully.

While you can *never* erase yourself from the police system after a DWI, you can minimize the hassle the system causes for you by acknowledging the mistakes you have made in the past and presenting yourself as someone who has reformed.

80. CREDIT APPLICATIONS

You remember that your credit score has suffered. This is true, but it goes deeper. On any credit applications you complete, you may have to say whether or not you have gotten a DWI. If you have and you lie, then they can impose a penalty on you, up to and including the cancellation of the credit line they have offered you. If you have used your credit line to pay for a mortgage or a car loan, this may mean that they take away your home or your car.

No one wants to pay a higher rate for a loan. Sometimes, however, you have no choice. If a lender won't provide you credit without charging you a higher rate, try to make up for it on the other side of things. When you are repaying your loan, pay a little more on each installment. This will help to minimize the compounding interest that will add up the longer the loan is active.

As you are paying more for your loan, think about the people who are *not* so fortunate to escape from a DWI with such minor ramifications. Brooke Lorenzen was only nineteen years old when she crashed on I-95 in Florida, killing Mario Bizier. She was drinking before she drove, registering a blood alcohol level of 0.11, but that was not the only cause of the crash.

Instead, Lorenzen's "D" was twofold. The other "D" was the same as the driver who killed Allie White: distraction. Lorenzen admitted that when she crashed into Bizier's vehicle, she was on her phone. She crossed from one lane to the next, striking a Mack 600 truck with her car, ending the life of a man whom many people in the area considered a close friend.

Lorenzen's case continues to work its way through the court system. Her charges, however, call for lengthy prison sentences, and when someone dies because of a DWI, the court is almost never lenient, even when it is a first offense and even when the driver is as young as Lorenzen.

CHAPTER IX

Every year, the number of DWIs increase. Despite the best efforts of educators and lawmakers, people continue to drive while drinking, while they are distracted, and while they are on drugs. One year has proven to be the exception to the rule. For that one year, the first time in a very long time, there were fewer DWIs.

It was *2020*.

Due to the COVID-19 pandemic, there was less driving. That meant fewer DWIs and fewer tickets. The year 2020 was the one time in all of our lives when the roads became a little safer. The problem was that *other* problems increased in place of DWIs. People were drinking more in their homes, which unfortunately resulted in an increase in the rate of domestic violence.

It took a *pandemic* to slow down the DWI rate. To me, that says a lot. It should not take an entire shutdown of our society to cut back on such a dangerous practice. Knowing what we know, we should be able to come together and learn to do better. We should be able to help each other to develop healthier habits.

That starts—and I believe this fully—with forgiveness and grace. Unless we forgive each other and show one another the charity we all deserve, we are not going to make any real changes within the system. We will make the same mistakes, maybe in different ways, and we will suffer most of the same consequences.

One woman I met told me about her horrific experience with a DWI. It was not hers but someone else's. A driver, who would later be charged with a DWI, struck her while she was driving early one morning. She not only lost her pregnancy in the resulting crash, but her husband in the passenger seat and her child in the back seat also died from their injuries. She showed up to my class because she wanted to understand what we needed to do differently. She wanted to learn what she could do to prevent the tragedy from striking anyone else ever again.

I could see there was *no* hatred in her eyes. Despite the loss she had suffered, she had forgiven the man who hit her and killed her entire family. If she can forgive them, then we can *all* find forgiveness in our own lives.

While that sinks in, let's review the next ten consequences of driving while impaired.

81. JOB APPLICATIONS

Every time you apply for a job, they frown on you because of your DWI. The job you could have done, you can no longer do. You go from holding a degree in something to being unable to find any work in your field of study. You have to go work at McDonald's or someplace like that. Although you may resist minimum-wage work at first, you may have no choice but to accept whatever job you can get.

There are, however, always skills you can learn to make some progress in your career. Coding is available to everyone, thanks to the internet. Watch some videos about web development and see if any of it sticks. If you can't stand computer work, then you may consider attending a trade school. Look into plumbing work, electrician work, and landscaping work. Each of these jobs will pay much more than minimum wage, and as long as you can do the job right, none of your customers are going to run a background check on you.

Instead of letting the *current* challenges of your DWI shape you, accept them for the temporary impediments they are and seek out the next big step forward.

82. LOW SELF-ESTEEM

People who have received a DWI commonly feel like they're no longer worthy to society anymore. They think about their dreams and sigh, convinced that they need to settle for whatever small joys they can get. Many people, if they are single or if their partners leave them, remain alone, never able to meet someone new because they think so little of themselves.

A pastor or a therapist will be most helpful for you if you can't snap yourself out of your negative emotions. Find someone like this who will listen without judgment and explain *why* you feel the way you feel. Talk about the mistakes you have made and the plan you have devised to avoid making those mistakes again. Whatever your pastor or therapist recommends that you do to heal yourself and leave the past behind you, do it.

When your self-esteem is low, it may seem counter-intuitive to entrust your major decisions to someone else. That is precisely what you have to do. Cede a little power so you can get some outside insight into your life.

83. DEPRESSION AND SUICIDAL THOUGHTS

People who have received a DWI may get suicidal too. Depression is a powerful, miserable force, and it can impact people in significant ways.

A young man came into my class once. He spent most of his time more often high than not, and he admitted that even after his DWI, he still wanted to get high. He felt like no one cared anymore; like no one would think anything of it if he died. After everything he had gone through, he felt like he would be better off dying to save everyone else the trouble of worrying about him, looking after him, or helping him manage his life after his DWI.

Managing your mental health in the wake of a DWI is of the utmost importance. Unlike so many other mistakes, which begin to clear up as soon as you have made them, a DWI will impose consequences on you over an extended period of time. As a result, you are at a higher risk for severe mental illness.

If you *ever* feel like you are considering harming yourself, reach out to someone. You can contact the National Suicide Prevention Lifeline, anytime, day or night, at 1-800-273-8255.

84. HOMELESSNESS

There are homeless people in every city. They live under the bridge, in the empty retaining ponds, at abandoned construction sites—they separate themselves from the rest of society. There are some people in your city right now who are homeless as a result of DWIs. They can't get a job; no one cares about them; and no one will give them an opportunity. They can't do anything to move themselves forward. Instead, they live their entire lives under a blanket or inside a tent. Without a shower, clean clothes, or a clean enough record, these people find themselves trapped in a vicious cycle of poverty.

There are a few specific things you can do to get yourself out of homelessness and back to your normal baseline.

1. Purchase a professional outfit or talk to a local organization that can provide one. This outfit is integral as you go on job interviews.
2. Locate the YMCA or YWCA near you. There, you can shower and shave before each job interview.

3. Be careful about the places you spend your time and the people you are around. While no one wants to spend the day alone, you may be doing yourself more harm than good if you are exposing yourself to people whose habits and goals don't align with your own.

85. EVALUATION

Your judge may tell you that to get your license back, you need to go through an evaluation. If this is the case, you must pay for a psychologist to meet with you and review your case. There will be several meetings during which he or she will build a profile of your psychology to determine whether or not you are a danger to yourself and to others. Your psychologist holds tremendous power over you, because he or she can decide at any time that the court should *not* trust you to drive or to reenter society.

Although this power can be intimidating, you need to make a positive impression on the psychologist. For that reason, try not to allow your interactions to overwhelm you. Keep things friendly, remain calm, and express to the psychologist your remorse for your mistake and your desire to live your life differently.

Psychologists *want* to help you. If you show them how much you've been working on improving yourself, that's what they need to see. Then, they can make a positive report to the court, and your evaluation should not hold you back during the post-DWI process.

86. JOB RESTRICTIONS

If your employer decides your DWI indicates you are not fit to do the job you were doing before, they may have to move you to a different role. For instance, if you operated a forklift in the past, your employer may prohibit you from doing so now. For construction workers, a DWI may mean a transition from high-paying technical work to more introductory tasks. Your pay may go from twenty dollars per hour to ten dollars per hour.

Keep in mind that DWIs are so common, you will probably be able to find someone at your workplace who has gone through the same thing. Even though you don't want to advertise your DWI, it helps to know you are not alone. If you can find an associate or superior who has recovered in their career from a DWI, try communicating with them discreetly for some job-specific advice during this process.

87. DRUG CHARGES

If you are driving while under the influence of drugs, or if there is cannabis in your possession when you get your DWI, you will face drug charges *in addition to* your DWI charge. While cannabis is legal in some states, in Texas, it is still considered an illegal drug. Drug charges will carry a stiffer penalty than they otherwise would have when they show up alongside a DWI. If both the DWI and the drug charge count as felonies, then you may be looking at *years* in prison. In many states, judges will take a harsh stance against defendants who have gotten a DWI while using illegal narcotics.

When you are facing more serious charges or even federal charges, it is even more important for you to enlist a high-quality attorney. While *no one* wants to break the bank to pay the fees these attorneys charge, you have to weigh those fees against the costs of a multi-year prison sentence.

Sometimes it may make sense to hire an attorney who specializes in drug charges rather than DWI charges, especially if the drug charges will carry a larger penalty. Your situation is unique. To determine the best course of action, start reaching out to qualified professionals for consultations.

88. DISTRACTION CHARGES

Even without drugs or alcohol, you may face severe penalties if you get into an accident. A judge may find that while your charge does not relate to drug use or drinking, your distraction is grave enough to merit "enhanced charges." This means if you are texting while you are driving, something similar to a DWI charge is within the realm of possibility.

Some of the *most* tragic cases have involved no drugs or alcohol at all. Texting and other forms of distraction *do* cost lives. Few people know this. If the "D" in *your* DWI is "distraction," then you can become a voice for this important cause. Let others know what has happened to you, so they too can learn from your mistake.

89. CRIMINAL RECORD

If you are charged with a felony, you can assume you are going to be paying for it for a long time. Even a decade into the future, you may find that your life still revolves around that one charge—that one night and that one mistake you made. Through it all, your criminal record will hang around your neck like a sign that distinguishes you in a way that you will not enjoy. Your DWI, no matter what anyone else tells you, is not going to come off your record. Once it is on there, it is on there forever. An attorney may take your money and seal the case, but a DWI will always show up on an FBI background check.

The strictest background checks are usually the most sensitive as well, involving government clearances or restricted information. If you know that a job will require an FBI background check, it is much better to tip off the hiring manager as to what they are going to find. Let them know about your situation so there are no surprises.

When in doubt, *choose transparency*. Saying nothing about a DWI that comes up on a background check puts you in a much more precarious situation than if you had been upfront about your mistake.

90. MADD

Mothers Against Drunk Driving (MADD) was formed to call attention to the issue of DWIs. As part of your restitution, you may have to meet with MADD. They will make you feel like you've killed their loved one, telling you how they felt when they lost a loved one or what they believe your actions say about you. To get your license back or to satisfy the judge's sentence, you *have* to listen to what they say.

After you have heard MADD's pitch, you may decide you want nothing more to do with them. On the other hand, their words and their mission may touch you, as they have touched me. In that case, ask them how else you can support them.

This advice goes for *any* nonprofit you encounter during the post-DWI process. Whenever you feel inspired to donate your time or money, do it. That feeling will set you off on a much more positive pathway than the one you have been on!

MADD was formed out of an awful tragedy. In May 1980, Candy Lightner received word that her daughter, thirteen-year-old Cari Lightner, had been killed in a car accident. As Candy recounts, "She was hit from behind, thrown 125 feet and left in the road to die. The drunk driver did not stop to render aid, nor did he tell anyone of his actions when he returned home. He did tell his wife 'not to look at the car' before passing out drunk. She ignored him, looked at the car, and the rest is history."

The driver was Clarence Busch. In 1980, when Busch and his choices cost the younger Lightner her life, laws around drunk driving were *not* the same as they are today. He had racked up three different DWI convictions in only four years, and because of the way the system worked then, he was able to keep his license. Even after

Lightner's death, Busch served only two years in prison. Within eighteen months, because of good behavior during his prison term, he was back into the world, and back into his vehicle, legally driving with full license privileges again.

Candy Lightner viewed this as a failing of the court system, and she took matters into her own hands. She founded Mothers Against Drunk Driving (MADD) to campaign for more severe penalties for DWIs. Whatever your feelings about your *own* situation, I would recommend that you make an effort to see things from Lightner's perspective. Imagine the heartache she felt and the gumption it took for her to turn that heartache into something positive.

Writing of her daughter, Candy Lighter said, "Cari always said she would never leave home because she 'had it made,' and always talked about going into the real estate business with me. She was a normal teenager, fretting over her weight, constantly on the phone, and the one everyone went to for advice. She was very mature for her age, and I still miss her. On the few occasions when I have dreamed of her, I wake up with the most incredible feeling of joy. I wish that would happen more often. I had to fight my way through the criminal justice system, or as we came to call it, 'the justice for the criminal system!'"

What can *you* take from your DWI experience? Instead of letting it get to another senseless tragedy like the death of Cari Lightner, how can you use this experience to make changes and do things better *now*?

Before you make any big decisions in response to that question, let me tell you a little more about how alcohol has touched my life too.

After I learned of my father's passing, I had to fly to Chicago to take care of all the funeral arrangements. Interestingly enough, it was the same funeral home that did Bernie Mac's funeral. At that point, I had not seen my father in years. He had never met my husband—who is my best friend—or my youngest son. Those meetings were to happen at our family reunion. My father never got the opportunity.

At the funeral home, I walked up to a back door. One of the employees stopped me.

"You don't want to go in there," she said.

I told her I was fine. My father was in there, and I was going to see him.

"You're not understanding," she insisted.

I started to get upset. Here I was, a forty-two-year-old woman, and this lady was telling me what to do. Her attitude seemed snippy, and she was keeping me from my late father. I am a sweet, good-natured woman. However, I do not let people push me around.

As I opened my mouth to protest again, the employee cut me off. "No, you don't understand," she told me. "He's deteriorated. It was hot here, and they found him a day or two late."

That was when it sunk in for me. If I walked through that door, everything would be different. I would remember him like that forever instead of holding on to the memories that we had made together.

I didn't go through that door. My father, who had died alone, remained alone.

That is what I want to help other people avoid. There is so much to learn here and so many pieces to this puzzle.

CHAPTER X

How do you view someone who has a DWI?

This is a valid question, and answers will vary from one person to another. Some people believe everyone who has gotten a DWI is an alcoholic. If you've been paying attention to what's written in this book, by now you know that should seem just a little too judgmental. Others may say those who have gotten a DWI are naive for believing they could get away with driving while impaired.

Compassion is the right course here, although that often requires significant effort. It's just perception. It's how we perceive each other. As I said at the start, I offer the items listed in this book without judgment. Every item means something different to each of us because our lives and our values are all different. Most times, when I share and consider this list, I make an effort to say I only want to point out how much money all of this can cost. It doesn't matter how much you make. Whether you make $25,000 or $250,000 a year, the consequences, fees, and charges add up, and they add up quickly.

One lady who came to my class, a teacher, was married to an immigrant. He got a DWI, and although she was on a teacher's salary, she had to hire the best attorney to keep him from getting deported. Keeping up with the attorney fees alone was a monumental struggle for her.

Another lady I met was the wife of a builder. Her husband received three DWIs, and these all but burned through their retirement fund. Every time she got a call from the police station, she knew their savings would drop again. She paid it, but after all of that, her husband couldn't even work as a builder anymore. Their lives were *different* because of his DWIs. Both she and her husband knew the cost and pain of putting out his fires all too well.

People react to DWIs differently. In most cases, people want to stay out of jail, and to do that they are willing to spend massive amounts of money. They will take out loans to cover legal fees, fines, classes, and anything else they must pay for to ensure another chance at freedom. Once they are back at home, they look over their bills and realize there is no realistic way they can pay for everything.

That is the consequence of playing with fire. More often than not, you get burned.

91. STEREOTYPED

If you get a DWI, people are going to stereotype you. I learned that one firsthand when I called a fellow instructor to see if I could sit in on his class. He immediately assumed I had received a DWI myself and spoke to me in a rude tone. He put me down and treated me like I was nothing, affording me a glimpse of what my time in his class would have been like if I had gotten a DWI.

It is disappointing when someone makes assumptions about who you are and what you are doing. Specifically, during the post-DWI process, you are going to meet people who are willing to write you off for a single mistake. They decide that because of one thing that has happened in your life, they know exactly who you are and what your value to society is.

Only *you* choose who you are and what your value is. No one can tell you what the future holds for you. If you are willing to work hard to move on from this mistake, there is little that is outside your grasp. Remind yourself every day that you are *more* than the unfair, incorrect stereotypes people hold about DWIs.

92. TRAIN ENGINEER

This may seem like an offbeat example, but it's true. A train engineer will definitely lose their license. You cannot have a DWI and continue to work as a train engineer. If you are unaware, those jobs pay *well*, requiring significant training and time investment. To go through all of that and then lose it is *devastating*.

This one was surprising to me, if only because I had never met a train engineer before I heard it. There is a more important underlying truth here. After you have gotten a DWI, you have to *prove* to people that they can count on you to perform technical tasks proficiently.

Try not to take this personally. People and organizations, such as those that manage the railroads, are only looking out for their own interests. If they refuse to hear you out and allow you to prove yourself, that is on them. On the other hand, if they *do* allow you to prove yourself, respect that opportunity and make the most of it.

93. PAROLE OFFICER

This is *not* the same thing as a probation officer. If you go to jail and then get out, then you have to pay for a parole officer. This person will check in on you and make sure you are sticking to the terms of your release. At any time, your parole officer can report you to the court, sending you back to jail to serve the remainder of your sentence. That will also entail an additional fee.

Parole officers work some of the most stressful jobs in law enforcement. They are under an enormous amount of pressure, and they have to handle sensitive cases. Keep in mind that if you run into a parole officer on their bad day, they may take some of their stress out on you.

As always, you will do best by *thinking collaboratively*. Ask yourself what you can do to make your parole officer's life easier, not harder. Clearly communicate your desire to work with them peacefully.

94. CIVIL LITIGATION

Independent of the court that tries you for your DWI, civil litigation will add to your woes. A victim may be suing you because you've killed their loved one, for example. In the case of a death, you have to pay a lot of money. Civil courts regularly pass judgments of six and seven figures in cases where someone who has gotten a DWI has also caused a death.

While civil court may not frighten people the way that criminal court does, the penalties are no less real. For that reason, I would advise that you do *not* skip out on hiring an attorney. It may be tempting to handle your own case when there is no jury to convince of anything, but it is no less difficult an undertaking.

The law is complex, and judges can be unforgiving of errors during a hearing. Save yourself the headache and enlist a professional's support during your civil case!

95. PRISON

Prison time is common for multiple DWIs. Someone I met had five DWIs, and for the last one, he went to prison for eight years. By the time he got out, he would have to pay parole to the tune of about $47,000. On top of that, he said during his time in prison, he bunked with someone who had committed a homicide. He learned the murderer in his cell had received *less prison* time than he did for his DWI—and his DWIs hadn't ever killed anyone. Once you have received one or two DWIs, the law becomes very narrow. Your chances of retaining freedom are usually lost. Repeat offenders almost always have to serve a prison sentence.

If prison is unavoidable for you, then try to make that time productive. Fitness and reading are the two most popular hobbies for prisoners. Set aside time for each of these things daily to keep your body and your mind sharp.

The *worst* choice you can make in prison is to let your negative self-talk overtake you. Instead of sinking into your worst emotions, cultivate positive habits to overcome them.

96. HALFWAY HOUSE

After you finish your prison sentence, you may not be able to go directly home. Instead, the court might want to make sure you are going to do okay outside the prison. You've been in prison for an extended period of time, which can lead to psychological or emotional challenges. To keep an eye on you, the court could mandate you to spend time in a halfway house. As you may guess, this is going to cost you money.

In a halfway house, you will meet people who are looking to change and people who are not. This is why you must choose your friends carefully. Anytime someone gives you a bad feeling or makes a negative impression, remain polite but try to separate yourself from them.

Since you want *your* halfway house story to mark the beginning of a new chapter, not the continuation of an old one, you should go about it intentionally. Think about all the value you can get out of this opportunity to get yourself back into regular society.

97. PAROLE

Parole, aside from the money it costs you, is also going to take up your time and keep you from other opportunities. If you are getting out of prison early, then your parole may match the remainder of your sentence plus some number of years. Those may feel like *lost years* because you are unable to do things that you would have been able to do if you weren't on parole.

Although support groups for parolees are rare, they do exist. You can also find other people who have gone through parole. In speaking with them, you may get an idea of the steps they took to work through their sentences successfully. Try to find *former* parolees, rather than current ones, as it is tough to say which of the current parolees is going to end up in the right place a year or two from now.

98. COMMUNITY SERVICE

There *will* be community service that goes along with your prison sentence and fines. Community service does not replace any of the other things you may be required to do, like take classes or deal with probation. If you serve time first, you'll still have to complete your community service and any other requirements when you get out of prison. If you try to skip it, the court system *will* come after you.

To make your community service easier on yourself, think of the good it is doing for other people. One way to drive this point home for yourself is to *journal about it.* I would advise journaling, in fact, about the entire post-DWI process. Write down your thoughts and feelings so they do not fester in your mind or fly under the radar in your subconscious.

Community service can *uplift you* as long as you are thinking about it the right way.

99. TIME

Most generally, you are losing your *time* when you get a DWI. You are missing out on days, weeks, months, and years because of all the many obstacles you will face. There is no way around any of it. When you get a DWI, when you are in that system, the only way out is through. That is all you can do. Follow the steps the court outlines for you, accept that it is going to be uncomfortable, and try to hold onto hope.

You can't get your time back. That is an immutable fact of life. However, you can make up for lost time by ensuring that you use the rest of your life for good things. Reflect on the parts of your life that are most meaningful to you, like your career, your friends, and family.

How do *you* want to think about your life when you have finished the post-DWI process?

What do *you* want to get out of this process?

Only you can answer these questions. In doing so, you can position yourself not only to avoid another DWI in the future, but to make sense of the choices that have led you to this one.

100. GRIEF

Throughout all of these obstacles and in their aftermath, grief is going to float over your head like a stormy cloud. You might even wish it would rain, but more often than not, you'll find this difficult feeling feeds the flames. Again, there is no getting out of it. The grief is there for you to address and for you to live with no matter what. Grief has no price tag. It costs you in a thousand ways you may never realize. A DWI can prevent you from living your best life. It will hold you back until you have dealt with it completely.

You *can't* ignore grief. There is simply no way. Sooner or later, you have to face up to the trauma of what you have lost. This is why it is best to face your grief head-on, dealing with it as soon as you notice it.

For especially challenging grief or emotions that are holding you back, try meditation. A pastor or a therapist will recommend the same thing. Every day, set aside five or ten minutes for silence, focusing on your breath as a respite from your stress.

Some time ago, there was a gentleman who came to my class twice. He told me he and a friend were going somewhere late at night. They were talking and paying almost no attention to the road.

The gentleman hit something. He and his friend argued about turning back. The gentleman said it sounded like something big, and his friend said it was a deer.

They did go back, and they found a teenager lying dead in the middle of the road. Drunk and high on drugs, the teenager had thrown himself in front of the car. Although both the gentleman and his friend were sober, they felt incredibly guilty about what had happened. That is how these things play out; the emotions follow people for years after the incidents occur.

UNDERSTANDING CONSEQUENCES
AND KNOWING COMPASSION

I store these stories like they're my own. There is a reason for that: I know how meaningful they are. When I meet someone and they tell me about their DWI, I feel like I have to listen to them. I have to commit their tales to memory so I can pass them along. That is my duty, the life I have chosen, because I know what it would mean to stop just one tragedy.

Because of my work, I read and hear about these tragedies all the time. I feel drawn to them, and I take them in, so I better comprehend the enormity of this undertaking. Every day, we can do better as a society, if we are all willing to work harder and to acknowledge our failings. That is what I hope you get out of this book. Don't *feel bad* about your past, and don't beat yourself up. However, *change your behavior*. Do something differently to avoid making the same mistakes again.

In 2017, Lauren Davis made a mistake that will stay with her for the rest of her life. She was drunk and on drugs when she crashed her vehicle. Two of the people in her car, a sixteen-year-old and a twenty-five-year-old, both died. It was *not* her first DWI.

Because of her history and the severity of the crash, a California district attorney charged Davis with murder in the second degree. That crash, which happened the night before Thanksgiving, changed multiple lives *permanently*. In late 2021, a judge sentenced Davis to fifteen years in prison. Davis, at the sentencing hearing, said, "I would give anything to take back what happened that day. It tears me to pieces that I can't, and it kills me every day."

Think about how *you* would feel if, instead of reading this book and hoping to get your life back on track because of a DWI charge, the guilt of two lost, innocent lives were on your shoulders as well.

Another woman, Alexandra Mansonet, was on the other side of the country a year before Davis's crash. Mansonet, driving on a residential New Jersey road, was neither drinking nor on drugs, but she *was* texting on her phone. According to recent New Jersey laws, she would be treated and sentenced as if she had been drunk driving.

This New Jersey woman is facing up to a decade in prison after being convicted in a groundbreaking case. She was texting while driving and killed a pedestrian in a state that now considers texting and driving just as serious as drunk driving. For killing thirty-nine-year-old Yuwen Wang, the pedestrian she hit with her vehicle, Mansonet was found guilty of murder in the second degree and sentenced to five years in prison.

The district attorney assigned to Mansonet's case explained that when the vehicle struck the pedestrian, the driver never hit her brakes or attempted to swerve. She was so distracted that she only knew she had hit someone *after* it was too late.

The next time you have had something to drink and consider getting behind the wheel of your car, or the next time you pick up your phone for a text while you should be watching the road, look around yourself and think about tragedy. Think about the people who are out there driving. Someone out there, maybe even in your town or city, has chosen to get behind the wheel and drive while under the influence. We can only hope they stay far away from anyone else, or better, that they reconsider and pull over. If they do that, then the potential tragedy awaiting them and their victims never becomes a story at all.

That is what I hope to accomplish. I want to prevent these stories from becoming your stories. When someone thinks about driving drunk, I want them to think back on my words here. I want them to remember the stories of woe that I have had to hear and share.

This book, I believe, could become a force for good in the world. I hope people think about the things we've discussed within these pages the next time they spend an evening in a bar or an afternoon in a friend's backyard. If you feel too drunk to walk in a straight line, remember the stories here. Remember the costs, the losses, and the penalties, and do something better.

When I go over these subjects in my class, I often stop at twenty or thirty items. It can become overwhelming, and I don't want to lose my students. Those who did hear the whole list, though, kept telling me that I needed to write a book. They understood what I was trying to say. A hundred wildfires merging and burning all around you feels like a lot no matter who you are.

One young woman in my class, a seventeen-year-old, never got a DWI. Her *brother* received the charge. Due to this, her parents had to spend the tuition money they'd been saving for her education on him instead. Not long after, her brother took his own life. That is a sad story, of course. My intention is not to cause anyone pain. I'm not trying to hurt anyone, and I'm not trying to offend anyone. In my class, I ask my students to forgive me for what I'm about to say. I ask the same of you. Forgive me for laying all of this information out there, as raw and as direct as I have.

We *need* to talk about these things. We need to get on the same page. I may say the word *blue*, but what does that bring to mind? You may think of the blue ocean, a river, or the sky. The person next to you might think of fruit, a particular pigment of paint, or feeling sad.

If I say the word *DWI*, what comes to mind?

Few are aware of how costly and damaging DWIs can really be.

Some people may start to make a list like mine, but no one's list is ever as long. They stop at five or ten items, unaware of how lengthy this list can become.

To lighten the mood, there is one story I like to tell in my class. It started on a morning like any other. I was on my way to teach my defensive driving class. I had always thought it would be *absurd* if I got hit on my way to teach my class.

That day, it happened. I was rear-ended very hard. I pull over alongside the gentleman who hit me. For as long as I've been teaching my class, I have to admit that I didn't pick up on the signs. He came up to my window and asked me if I was okay. I told him to give me a moment, as I was still in shock. I called the police and told them the same thing: my car had been hit from behind, and I was in shock.

I asked the driver if he had his license. He told me that he *had* had it, but that he had dropped it.

My next question was if there was anything else I needed to know. He was incoherent, but he showed me his insurance card before driving off and leaving the scene. He just left me standing there. Finally, the police arrived. I let them know that I had gotten the gentleman's information but that he had left.

The next thing I knew, I saw the gentleman driving back—and on a bare rim! The police officer, still holding my license, went chasing after him. Another police officer took me to my class.

There were nineteen students waiting for me. They all saw me, the tow truck, and the damaged car. *That* was a fun story to tell!

Later that day, the police officer met up with me to return my license. I asked him what was going on, and he told me that there were pills in the gentleman's car. Due to the presence of those narcotics, the gentleman received a DWI.

A week later, I went to rent a replacement car as, of course, mine was in the shop for repairs. Who do I see standing in line but *the same gentleman*. He didn't appear to recognize me, but I recognized him immediately.

I tell that story because it stands out as *funny*, and so few of these stories do. Every time I teach my class, someone cries. Someone admits they have a DWI. It always happens, at least once during the class, or they wait until after the class, then unburden themselves and share their story with me.

There is no single demographic that gets DWIs or is immune to them. I have taught the rich and the poor. I've taught the CEOs of companies and people who work for minimum wage. Many people who get a DWI end up running their own businesses because it's tough to find employers who will overlook such a transgression.

I believe in charity, and I believe in forgiveness. Another man lost the love of his life when a drunk driver killed his fiancée. A decade went by, and all those feelings could have burned a hole through his heart. Instead, after the driver served his time in prison and was released, he fell in love and invited the man to attend his wedding. Although shocked, the man—his victim—showed up to the wedding motivated by compassion and forgiveness.

At the time of writing this book, there is one relevant case everyone is talking about: Nicole Linton. A traveling nurse based in Houston, she was working in Los Angeles when she blew a red light going more than one hundred miles per hour in a Mercedes and killed six people including a pregnant mother and an infant. This tragedy is heartbreaking on many fronts. There are people, children, who are dead and whose families' lives will never be the same. As well, there is a nurse, someone who committed her life to caring for others, who will likely never get out of prison.

Can we find forgiveness? Can we find *peace* in our hearts, as we know God does for us, to see people past the mistakes they have made?

Love is what drives me. If you have gotten a DWI, it's in the past as soon as you have paid your fines and made your restitution. You get a second chance, with me at least. Every time you consider driving after you've ingested drugs or alcohol, and every time you consider driving with a cell phone in your hand, you have a chance to make the right choice, improve your life, and keep the lives of others safe. You never have to drink and drive or drive distracted. There is always a choice, and I hope this book has empowered you to make the right one. Even if emotions rarely come into play for you, the unbelievable costs associated with putting out the flames of your DWI are as prohibitive and damaging as they can be.

Sometimes, people get lucky. Senator Sandra Cunningham of New Jersey could have fared much worse from her DWI charge. After hitting multiple parked cars and failing a field sobriety exam, she had to defend herself against a felony DWI case. It was only because of legal technicalities that Senator Cunningham was able to beat the original charge and negotiate it down to simple reckless driving, a misdemeanor.

Do *not* bank on this sort of luck. Instead, take action right now. Ask yourself what you can do to live more responsibly and what it means to you to become a positive, productive member of society. While your outlook today may seem bleak, it *is* possible. For all of the sad stories that I have heard, I have met many people who have recovered from their DWIs, only to live an even better life than they had before.

It's possible. I want that better life for *you*. While never getting a DWI is the best way to avoid these consequences, if you have one, work your way through the process, whatever you, the judge, and your advisors have drawn up. Wisdom, in time, will come to you, and hopefully this book has provided you with an illuminating head start.

Your life is going to come at you much more rapidly than you ever expect it to. At the same time, if you put yourself in a position where you have to deal with a DWI, it may all come at you even *more* rapidly—in the blink of an eye. That is something I hear from my students constantly. They tell me that it seems like they can split their lives into two halves, one half before the DWI and one half after it.

What you do with the half of your life after your DWI is completely up to you. You may feel like the circumstances that have led you to drinking, drugs, or distraction have been outside of your control. I am not here to tell you otherwise. All that I am here to tell you is that you can decide in this moment that you are going to do things differently. Whether or not things have been your fault in the past, your life today is your responsibility. I know this information can change things for the better because I have *seen it* do exactly that.

I have seen students show up to my classes seemingly unprepared to learn anything at all. Then, when we get to talking, I tell them about the stories I have heard, and I tell them about all the consequences they haven't had to face yet. When I explain to them that as bad as their life seems today, it can get that much worse, they usually start to listen.

Don't let your situation get so awful that an instructor like me is using it as an example in class. Don't force someone to explain to you how much worse things could be. Instead, choose to acknowledge that in this moment, things are bad and you need to do something about them. A DWI charge, even when there is no decade-long prison sentence attached to it, should serve as a wake-up call to you.

One of the hardest parts about my job as a defensive driving instructor is finding a balance between pointing out my students' faults and pointing out my students' strengths. Believe me when I say that no one who has ever shown up in my class was *just* their DWI charge. There are no drunk drivers in my classes. On the contrary, there are people who have driven drunk. There are also no drug addicts in my classes, but there are people who have been addicted to drugs.

You are more than the sum of the worst mistakes you have made. You are a better person than people would assume you are on the worst day of your life. If you won't believe in yourself right now, then let me do it for you first. I believe in you. You are somebody, and you don't need to set your life on fire.

What position are you in right now? What is *your* struggle?

Life is different for each of us. Yet, through empathy, we can understand what others are going through. Even if you have never gotten a DWI or heard about another DWI experience before you started reading this book, you could imagine the stress that it would cause. You could *feel* the discontent it could create in someone's life.

If you are navigating the post-DWI process, words may provide only minor solace. You think about the money you have to pay, the work you have to do, and the time you have to wait to get your life back on track. As someone who has stood beside thousands of people going through the same thing, trust me when I say that it *gets better*.

A few years from now, after you have paid your restitution or gone through a class like the one I teach, you may feel that you have grown from this struggle. *Then* it will be much easier for you to give yourself the love and respect you deserve, to make real, meaningful changes to your life, and to *thrive*, no matter what has happened in your past.

Faith is the substance of things hoped for,
the evidence of things not seen.
—Hebrews 11:1

"IN THE MIDDLE"

I look to my left and then I look to my right only to find out I
am in the middle.
Where do I go from here? I look up and then I look down and
still I am not level to this ground, in the middle.
Precious gold and silver exist but I have none.
Rumors and rumors of wars are happening all around me.
Am I any help?
Speak, scream, or holler but does anyone hear me?
The body, the mind, and the soul want to be free.
I exist; I am here; do you not see me?
I have a voice; I am not dead; I am alive.
I am in the middle for a reason to help both sides.
You may not know me, you may not see me, but I am here for
a purpose.
Salvation and Meditation are Equalization to Power.
1 to the right that's Grace; 1 to the left that's Mercy; and 1 in
the middle—That's ME.

—LADONNA CLAUDE

ABOUT THE AUTHOR

LaDonna Claude is the mother of two sons and two daughters, as well as the grandmother of four and a loving wife. She serves as a Certified Defensive Driver Instructor and also does public speaking engagements and other outreach initiatives in her community. Her driving passion is for spreading awareness and educating people about the three Ds of DWI: distraction, drugs, and drinking.

Through her classes, LaDonna has guided others toward healthier habits and safer driving practices. She draws on her own past, including experiences with her father, who passed away at an early age due to alcohol abuse, to make her lessons relatable and meaningful.

SYNOPSIS

As a defensive driving instructor, LaDonna Claude has guided her students through the post-DWI process, teaching them not only how to get back on the road but how to reclaim their lives. In this book, she explains a hundred different things that people should consider when navigating this process. She lends invaluable advice and insights into the realities of the system, recalling memorable, touching stories along the way.

Made in the USA
Middletown, DE
26 February 2023

25407498R00068